LIFE IS CALLING

Life Is Calling

By Travis Clark

Charleston, SC
www.PalmettoPublishing.com

Life Is Calling

Copyright © 2020 by Travis Clark
All rights reserved

ISBN: 978-1-64990-705-9

Table of Contents

Dedicated to my love, Jena.
There is no way that this book is written without you.

Introduction:
It's Time to Change Your
Web Browser

"Life is full of surprises when we choose wonder over security."
—Unknown

"Do not follow where the path may lead. Go instead where there is no path and leave a trail." —Ralph Waldo Emerson

Once upon a time, you believed that *anything* was possible.

Do you remember?

There was a day that you were full of so much wonder and imagination that you would turn your bib around backward, and it wasn't a bib any longer; it had transformed into a cape because you were a superhero. There was a day that you had the sort of imagination that you could look at dirty flip-flops and turn them into ruby slippers. There was a day that you were confident that you would be a professional basketball player even though no one in your family is taller than 5' 7".

So what happened?

I recently saw this cartoon the other day of two children playing blocks together, and the caption underneath has one of the children asking the other: "What do you want to do when you give up?"

"What do you want to be when you give up?"

When did we begin to believe that growing up was synonymous with *giving up*? When did we start to think that the point of life is to arrive safely at death? How is it that although we were all born one-of-a-kind-originals, that far too many people die a carbon copy of someone else's life?

My daughter, Finley, is about three years old, and she recently started putting on one of her "fancy hats" and walking into a room and, with both arms in the air, she yells, "TA-DA!" I didn't teach her to do this, and neither did my wife. We didn't sit her down one day and tell her that this is how the Clark family enters rooms. This was birthed purely out of the imagination and whimsy of a childlike spirit.

I'm not suggesting that this is how you should walk into work tomorrow. However, that would be a pretty great way to make an entrance. But what I wonder is this: when and why did we stop engaging life with this sort of wonder? When and why did we stop walking into our lives with both hands in the air, declaring, "TA-DA?" When and why did we stop believing deep in our bones that anything was possible?

And to answer this question, we will need to ask another critical question: what web browser do you use?

I bet you didn't see that one coming, did you?

Stay with me. I promise that I have a point.

See, discovering why you might be trading creativity for conformity could be as simple as identifying what web browser you use. At least, according to an interesting study from Organizational Psychologist Adam Grant, in his book "Originals."

In it, he shares a study that predicted your job performance and your commitment to your job, just by knowing the web browser you use. The results showed that Firefox and Chrome users significantly outperform Internet Explorer and Safari users.

Why? It's not a technical advantage. The four groups, on average, have similar typing speeds and similar levels of computer knowledge. They discovered in this study that it wasn't an issue of competence but an issue of *curiosity*. It's about how you got the browser that you use. Because if you use Internet Explorer or Safari, those browsers came preinstalled on your computer, which means you accepted the default option. If you wanted Firefox or Chrome, you had to be curious enough to doubt the default, believe there was something better, and then purposefully search for that better web browser.[1]

You might conclude that this has no existential implications. It is just a web browser, after all, right? But I can't help but wonder if this is not a microcosm

---

[1] I remember when I first read this study. I immediately called my wife and asked her what browser she uses. She then told me that she uses Safari, and I, the competitive fool that I am, said to her that I use Chrome and therefore am, according to this study, more creative than her. Little did I know, but she was having a terrible day before this call, and the last thing she needed to hear was that I was better than her. She then started to cry. I felt like such a tool.

of the same battle many of us face as we decide how to spend this one life that we have been given.

Far too many people accept the default and never experience what could be because they believe that *what is* is all that there is. So you trade curiosity for conformity and your destiny for the default. As a result, the one-of-a-kind-original dies a carbon copy.

It turns out that although curiosity may kill the cat, that it very well may be the key ingredient that leads humans to a fuller life.

Adam Grant later suggests that if you can fight to remain curious that you open yourself up to the opposite of déjà vu. There's a name for it. It's called *Vuja de.*

The Vuja de moment is the reverse of the French saying - Déjà vu, which means "already seen it." Vuja de is when you look at something that you have already seen but decide to look at it with a different perspective, and you choose to challenge the status quo.

Vuja de is like the screenwriter who looks at a movie script that can't get the green light from any production companies. And in every past version of this movie script, the main character has been an evil queen. But then the screenwriter, Jennifer Lee, starts to question whether that makes sense. She doubts the default. Her curiosity leads her to challenge the status quo. So she rewrites the first act, reinventing the main character from an evil queen into a tortured hero. As a result, the movie Frozen becomes the most successful animated movie ever with the most annoying song ever.[2]

Wayne Dyer said, "If you change the way you look at things, the things you look at change."

---

2   Okay, okay. I kind of like the song and I hate that about myself.

That is Vuja de.

And that is why I have spent over six years studying and writing about the Hebrew man, Abraham, and the moment he heard the whisper of life beckon him, and he said "yes." Little did Abraham know, but he would be offering all of humanity an example of what it looks like to approach life with curiosity and what it looks like to tap into Vuja de. I think that's why his story has prevailed for over three thousand years.

It has prevailed because the story of his curiosity gave the world permission to be curious. Abraham's courage to follow life when it called pioneered a new way to be human that the world had never known before. When understood for the revolutionary story that it is, Abraham's story is not just a story for those who identify with the Jewish, Muslim, or Christian traditions. Abraham's story is for all people because Abraham's story is *our story*. He is a symbol of what it will take to live your fullest life as your truest self.

Abraham was a seventy-five-year-old Mesopotamian man who decided to doubt the default and allow curiosity and faith to lead him forward. Abraham heard life call him forward, and he said, "yes."

And I believe that life is calling you as well.

I believe that on the other side of the default is a destiny awaiting you.

This book is about providing language to the divine voice that has been whispering hopes and dreams within you. This book is for those who are ready to say "no" to the default so that they can begin to say "yes" to their destiny. This book is for those who are craving to reengage that childlike whimsy and wonder for life because deep down, they know that this is not all there is.

So throughout the next nineteen chapters, we're going to unpack the story of Abraham. What you'll discover is a human who faced family turmoil, fear, insecurity, and risk and persevered because although the cost of following life into the unknown was great, he knew that the cost of staying where he was was greater. As a result, Abraham experienced the fullest life as he became his truest self.

I have broken down Abraham's story and our journey together into three sections: *The prison of existence, the path of the curious, and the promise of life.* We'll travel through each section, and I hope that you will move from the prison of existence, trek the path of the curious and begin to experience the promises of life by the end of this book.

But here's my only request.

Please bring your whole *authentic self* into this journey. [3]

You cannot fake your way into a fully alive life. Full life belongs to those with the courage to hold their whole lives, the good and the messy parts, with open hands. During our time together, I will be sharing some of the most vulnerable parts of my life. Like you, I don't want to settle for *what is* and miss out on *what could be.* So I am asking you to do the same. The story of Abraham is one that invites us into our fullest life by becoming our truest self. You will never become your truest self until you confront the false-selfs that exist within you.

All I ask is that you bring your whole self into this journey, and I promise that I will do the same.

Deal?

You might be asking why I am qualified to teach you how to live your fullest life by becoming your truest self. Well, the truth is, I don't know if I am, and

---

3 The brilliant Brené Brown once said that the true definition of courage is "to tell your whole story with your whole heart." I love that. This is the sort of courage you will need to follow life where it is calling you.

that's not why I decided to write this book. But I do know what it feels like to be faking my way through life instead of living it fully. I do know what it feels like to be wounded and unsure if I could move forward. The feeling of fear and insecurity is a real struggle that I still battle even to this day.

But I also know the hope and wonder that has come with saying "yes" to life when it calls, even when it isn't easy. I know what it's like to pack your existential bags and leave where you have always been to pursue where you must go.

So I don't write this book as someone with all of the answers. As a matter a fact, this book may spark more questions than answers for you. I hope it does. I write this book as a fellow traveler in this life and as someone, just like I believe you are, that does not want to waste this gift of life.

Because of this, you will find that I tend to ask a lot of questions throughout the following chapters. The reason for that is because I have not written this book to tell you what to think. As a pastor, I hear far too many books, blogs, and sermons that want to tell you what to think, and I'm not sure that it's always beneficial. Instead, I have written this book to help you create space to discover *how to think* through questions and introspection. This doesn't mean I won't share my opinion. I will. I'm an Enneagram 8, so sharing my opinion comes pretty naturally, ask my wife. But feel free to wrestle or disagree with it as you listen to what the voice of life wants to say to you.[4]

If you are reading this book and you would not call yourself a "believer" of any particular tradition of faith, I am so glad that you are reading, and I hope I haven't lost you. I'm not sure how you got this book, but I am so happy that you did. I want you to know that although I wrote this book from the perspective of faith in the God described in the pages of the ancient

---

4 Richard Rohr once said that "far too many pastors go years telling people *what to think* instead of creating space for people to discover *how to think*." I agree. I think *certainty* might be one of the main hindrances to people growing in life. Curiosity is sacred.

scriptures, I believe the tensions, concepts, and takeaways are relevant regardless of what you think about faith, God, and the Bible. I promise that you don't need to believe in God or even like pastors to get something from this book.

As we journey through the prison of existence, the path of the curious, and the promise of life, I believe you will be closer to a fuller life by becoming your truest self. So let's follow the whisper of life together and see where it takes us.

Are you ready to bring your whole self into this?

You shook on it earlier. So there is no going back now.

Let's do this.

Part One:
The Prison of Existence

Chapter 1

Soul Cycle, Purpose, and Why Tacos are Spiritual

"Two roads diverged in the wood, and I took the one less traveled, and that has made all the difference."—Robert Frost

"What if there really are two paths? I want to be in the one that leads to awesome."—Kid President

_____ is alive for a reason.

Go ahead and write your name in the line above. I'll be here when you're done.

Ready? Awesome.

I know you may not believe what you just wrote yet. It's okay. I get it. I haven't always believed it for my life either. If I'm honest with you, my relationship with this idea of purpose has been a fickle one. It seems like I am in one of these phases when it comes to living out my purpose. This perpetual cycle looks something like this:

Phase 1: "I have purpose!"
Phase 2: "Wait. Purpose is scary."
Phase 3: "Maybe I don't have purpose."
Phase 4: "Purpose is crap."

Phase 5: "I am crap."
Phase 6: "Okay, maybe I'm overthinking this."
Phase 7: "Dang it, purpose. I can't quit you!"
Phase 8: "Yay! I have a purpose!"
And repeat.

Ever been there? What phase are you in right now?

I've discovered that pursuing your purpose can feel a lot like going to a class at SoulCycle. If you've gone to SoulCycle or any other one of these cult-like cycling classes, you know what I mean.[1] But if you've never experienced Soul Cycle, let me explain.

When you walk in, the entire environment is intoxicating. From the overly enthusiastic people at the front desk to the super fit people coming out of their classes dripping in sweat and laughing. Before you even get on the bike, you're ready to punch this class in the metaphorical face. You start strong for the first two songs. The thumping bass and dark lighting have you jacked up. But then you start to feel the burn; it seems like everyone else is doing just fine, and by the time you get to the third song, you begin to wonder why you just paid an ungodly amount of money to do this to yourself. But then something happens. By song five, you hit a second wind because they started playing that old school hit, "Firework," by Katy Perry, and you refuse to be a bag blowing in the wind. You will beat this! And by the cool down, you are one of the sweaty people laughing as you leave the class, and whether you were the best in the class or just proud that you made it without throwing up—you now feel like you can do anything you set your mind to.[2]

Yeah. That's kind of how my relationship with purpose feels.

---

1   Shout out to the best SoulCycle instructor, Stephanie Peters. I'm not sure what I did to make you want to bring to the brink of death in your class. But I'm sorry.
2   I expect some sort of kickback for that serious mini-commercial for SoulCycle.

What about you? Does the idea of purpose fill you with hope, or does it press every button of insecurity you have? Maybe it does a little bit of both.

I have a love–hate relationship with purpose. I love it because, well, it's purpose, and who doesn't want in on some of that action? But I hate it because it turns out that the journey called "purpose" can be painful at times, and it is anything but linear or predictable. Purpose is anything but easy. If it were easy, then we wouldn't have a multi-billion dollar industry that exists solely to tell you and teach you how to discover your purpose.

Using the phases above as a metric, maybe you're at phase 1 and ready to punch fear in the throat. Or maybe you're at phase 3, 4, or 5 and ready to call it quits. Wherever you find yourself in that process, I hope you know that you're not alone and that somehow I can encourage you that purpose is worth the pain it will inflict. And I'm confident that you know this and you won't quit on purpose—because whether or not we agree on faith, on politics, that country music is the worst (it is), or that the Golden State Warriors are God's team (they are), I bet we can at least agree on this:

Humans were created for purpose.

Humans were created to create. Think about it. I had to be taught how to do math. I had to be taught how to drive a car. And every time I go to a wedding I am still taught how to dance.[3] But no one had to teach you how to dream and to be curious and to have aspirations. Those things were baked into your humanity, and whether we look at the ancient Mesopotamians who created the wheel 5,500 years ago, those creating world-shaping technology in Silicon Valley, or the barista who made latte art that looks like a unicorn, it is undeniable that humans were created to create.

---

3 Gloria Estefan said the "rhythm is going to get you." Well, Gloria lied to me because it has not gotten me yet.

But this is a double-sided coin. It is a beautiful thing when humans create. But on the other side of the coin, this means that when we stop creating, we are settling for a life that is beneath our humanity.

When you stop creating and stop living from purpose, you become *less human*.

Maybe you've never thought of it that way, but I am confident that you actually do believe this to be true. Something in you knows that no human being was created to just exist. Something in you knows that to stop creating, to stop dreaming, and to stop living intentionally is, in some very real and sad way, *subhuman*. I bet, no matter how many times you've gone through phases 3 to 5, that you eventually make it right back to phase 6.

Why keep doing that to yourself? Why do we keep signing up for this class called "purpose" even though we know it will be one of the hardest and most excruciating things we do?

My guess is that it is because we are humans and we just can't shake this feeling that we are here to create.

Did you know that, in the Hebrew Scriptures, the writers teach that from the beginning, all humans were created to be co-creators with God?[4] Now that may or may not be news to you. But this was an absolutely shocking deviation from the second most widely known creation story in the ancient world called the Enuma Elish, written about the seventeenth century BC. And according to the Enuma Elish, humans were created by the chief god, Marduk, not as co-creators, not as partners, and not as purpose-filled people. No, according to this creation story, humans were created as cheap slave labor for the disgruntled gods, who were tired of work.

---

4 Genesis 1:28

Think of the worst boss you've ever worked for and then make that boss the god and creator of the universe. Yeah, the god Marduk was sort of like that.

But then the Hebrew people started telling a totally different and totally new story about why humans came to be and what God was like. They said that this God, Yahweh, didn't create humanity to be slaves but to be co-creators. This account even said that we were created in this God's image. Meaning they believed that all people were created by a creative God, and we are made to mirror what this God is like to the world. So just as God loves, we love. Just as God stands against injustice, we do the same. And just as God creates—you guessed it—we create. And when we do these things, we project what God is like to the world.

Have you ever thought of creativity as spiritual?

I've always been taught that reading the Bible, praying, and singing worship songs on Sunday were the "spiritual" things. But according to the Hebrews, this was only scratching the surface. Because we were created to create, anything we create that makes a better world and mirrors what God is like is a profoundly *spiritual* act.

This means:
Creating art is spiritual.
Innovating new technology is spiritual.
Telling a great story through writing or theater is spiritual.
Raising children to be good humans is spiritual.
Making the perfect taco is spiritual.
I mean, who doesn't feel like they've encountered the divine when eating tacos? Can I get an amen?[5]

So according to the Hebrews, because we were created by a creative God, this means every creative endeavor we make is a spiritual act, whether it's

---

5 I feel God in every Taco Bell I enter.

labeled "Christian" or not. Which means one of the most spiritual things you do every day isn't to pray or to read the Bible. And don't get me wrong, I'm for those things. But what all of this means is that one of the most spiritual things you will do every single day is *choose.* Because every day you and I have the choice as to what we will create, and the question is, does it mirror to the world what God is like? Does your creative act nudge the world in a better direction?

Have you ever seen a movie and the story just did something deep within you? I remember the first movie that almost made me cry was *Armageddon* featuring Ben Affleck and Bruce Willis. I remember sitting there as a kid and watching Bruce Willis sacrifice his life on that asteroid. I can feel you judging me. I was just a young boy. My heart wasn't ready for that sort of loss.[6]

Or have you listened to a song and found yourself getting emotional?[7]

Or taken the first bite of that meal, and it felt like time stood still for just a moment because the food you just ate was *that* good?[8]

Do these things happen just because movies are entertaining, music is catchy, and food is delicious? Or do we do it because, when we encounter deep and real creativity that someone poured their heart into, it is almost like our souls bursts with joy because our souls remember what we were created for even if we might have forgotten. I wonder if we all love creativity because it reminds us of what it means to be human.

To the Hebrews, a fundamental part of what it meant to be human is to mirror the creativity of God in the world as God's co-creator. They didn't believe that God placed humans in a world just so we could keep the grass mowed and flowers watered. Instead, this God placed the first humans in a

---

6 Don't even get me started with the first 20 minutes of the movie "Up." It gets me every time.

7 "In the arms of an angel" by Sarah McLachlan. It gets me every…single…time.

8 Once again, Taco Bell.

world bursting at the seams with raw potential so that, together with God, we could create a future worth living in. That was the origin of the human story, and it painted a far more beautiful picture of hope and wonder than the Enuma Elish. Which, of course, is why the Hebrews creation story was jaw-dropping, head-turning, and mind-blowing news in the ancient world.

So the question we have to ask then is, could this story about humans still be true?

Is the world still bursting with potential, and is God still inviting us to partner with Him to create a better future?

Could it be true that we were created to create and a life that stops creating is not much of a life after all? It's just *existence*. And if this is true, then is the day we die not the day our heart stops but the day we stop creating a future? Is it the day we stop seeing our lives as a creative act to nudge the world forward into a better place?

I wonder if this is why we have a word that we use to describe a murderer, someone who literally ends someone else's future.

We say that person is *inhumane.*

Because when we stop creating or if we stop someone else from creating, we are actually existing beneath our humanity. We're *inhumane.* We understand the concept of 'inhuman,' which suggests an unspoken—but very real—consensus on what it means to be human. To be human is to create and to stop that creative process in you or someone else is what it means to be inhuman.

Now, rewind 2,000 years ago to a Middle Eastern rabbi named Jesus.

At one point in his ministry, Jesus taught that he came so that we could live a "full life."[9] For much of my life, I assumed that Jesus was talking about life *after* death. After all, it seemed that the majority of the sermons I heard as a kid all seemed to suggest that God's biggest priority is my life after death—and not so much my life *before* death.[10] Almost as if the whole point of this life is to simply endure it so that one day we can escape it. But when you read the words and teachings of Jesus, you can't help but wonder if we have misunderstood what Jesus came to show us. Because what becomes so clear when you look at the life of Jesus is that he was far more interested in you having life before death, not just life after death—because this life was always meant to be *lived*, not *endured*.

What if life was meant to be enjoyed, not escaped?

Jesus even said this about why he came in Luke 4:18: "The Spirit of the Lord is upon me, for he has anointed me to bring Good News to the poor. He has sent me to proclaim that captives will be released, that the blind will see, that the oppressed will be set free."

I don't know what you've been told about Jesus and what thoughts and images comes to mind when you hear that name, but I want you to know that the Jesus the Bible talks about is fighting for your future and always has been. While religion says it's all about what you do to get to God, Jesus came with a radical message about a God who could be found moving heaven and earth to get to *you*. This God was nothing like Marduk of the Enuma Elish or any of his fellow gods. He isn't looking for slaves to do his bidding. This God doesn't need something from you; he just wants something *for* you. This God is fighting for the future of those

---

9 John 10:10

10 If you have ever gone to a Christian summer camp, then you know what I'm talking about. I can't tell you how many times I've heard camp speakers say that they are trying to "scare the hell out kids." Yet, they fail to address how a theology about a God that has to threaten you because He loves you doesn't work. Anyone with a semi-healthy marriage knows this.

Who feel they have nothing to offer,
Who have ever been held captive by something,
Who have ever lost sight of their value,
Who have ever been oppressed by someone or something,
And anyone who has not been able to shake that they are filled with purpose.

So, I guess you could say that God is fighting for the future of...*everyone*.

He is a God of the prison break.[11]

This prison is called existence, and it's crowded. But God has blown the cell doors open in order to set humanity free to be fully human again. Because before you are any label that you may wear or has been given to you, you are, first and foremost, a human.

And every human is created to create.

And your most important creative act will be the future you create with your life.[12]

Maybe you've been waiting on the future, but can I let you in on a secret? The future is waiting on *you*. Your destiny isn't a destination; it's a decision. The prison door has been unlocked, and it's up to you to decide whether you'll stay inside or walk out and create a life that creates life for others.

I believe that life is calling all of us out of the prison called existence.

I believe that life is calling you.

The question is, will you answer?

---

11 Ah, Prison Break. A very underrated TV show.
12 For more thoughts on this, I really enjoyed Erwin McManus's book, "The Artisan Soul."

Chapter 2

The Divine Deconstruction Project

"The Lord had said to Abraham, 'Go from your country, your people and your father's household to the land I will show you. I will make you into a great nation, and I will bless you; I will make your name great, and you will be a blessing. I will bless those who bless you, and whoever curses you I will curse; and all peoples on earth will be blessed through you.'"—Genesis 12:1-3

"The terrible thing, the almost impossible thing, is to hand over your whole self—all your wishes and precautions—to Christ. But it is far easier than what we are all trying to do instead. For what we are trying to do is to remain what we call 'ourselves', to keep personal happiness as our great aim in life, and yet at the same time be 'good'. We are all trying to let our mind and heart go their own way—centered on money or pleasure or ambition—and hoping, in spite of this, to behave honestly and chastely and humbly. And that is exactly what Christ warned us you could not do. As he said, a thistle cannot produce figs. If I am a field that contains nothing but grass-seed, I cannot produce wheat. Cutting the grass may keep it short: but I shall still produce grass and no wheat. If I want to produce wheat, the change must go deeper than the surface. I must be plowed up and re-sown."—C.S. Lewis

Besides Jesus, Abraham is arguably the most influential person who has ever lived, and you didn't even know it. Did you know that Abraham is considered the spiritual ancestor of 2.4 billion Christians, 1.6 billion Muslims and 13 million Jews? To put it in perspective, that is more than half the people alive today. Yet what is so unique about Abraham's fame is that Abraham ruled no empire, he commanded no great army, and he performed zero miracles, and if I'm honest, the dude was a hot mess sometimes.

So here's the question we should be asking: why is Abraham such a big deal?

To answer that question, I first need to tell you a story from a man named Gordon Mackenzie.

Gordon worked at Hallmark for thirty years, and he did a lot of creative workshops in elementary schools. He wrote about one observation he had in a fantastic little book called *Orbiting the Giant Hairball*. Gordon wrote how he would start one of his workshops by asking all of the kids in the classroom a very simple question: "How many artists are there in the room?"

He would then invite those who would readily proclaim themselves to be artists to raise their hands. What was interesting to Gordon was how the patterns of responses never varied. When first graders heard the question, the entire class would raise their hands and wave them like a bunch of maniacs with Capri Sun pumping through their veins. When second graders were asked the same question, only about half the kids would raise their hands. When he got to the third graders, they would respond a little more casually with about one third of them raising their hands. But by the time he got to the sixth-grade class and Gordon asked how many artists were in the room, every time, without fail, only one or two would slowly and self-consciously raise their hands.

Gordon Mackenzie observed that over time that these students—who at one point in their lives, proudly and confidently saw themselves as artists—slowly began to see themselves in more standard and sanitized terms. Slowly but surely, they would begin to choose *conformity* over creativity. Gordon later observed in his book that society over time seems to be making people less creative, not more. And for years now, Gordon Mackenzie said a statement that has haunted me since I first read it:

"From the cradle to the grave, the pressure is on: Be normal."

You see, at some point, it appears that people begin to believe the lie that there are creative people and then there are rest of us.

But have you ever noticed that no one has to teach a child how to be creative? There is no class for that. And no one ever teaches a child how to color outside the lines. The problem is that, somewhere along the way in this life, we are taught to color *inside* the lines. The problem is that we are taught how *not* to be creative.

And as a result, we trade creativity for conformity.
We trade wonder for safety.
We trade making a life for making a living.
And over time, we stop raising our hands because we stop seeing ourselves as an artist.

Yet what the creativity and imagination of every child should teach us is that our souls in their default state are designed to dream. We were wired for wonder. Our souls are created for more than we know. But the risk that we all face is that, as we get older, somewhere along the way, we lose our imagination and substitute it with standardization.

And I am convinced that this is the reason Abraham's story has mattered to 2.4 billion Christians, 1.6 billion Muslims, and 13 million Jews.

Let me explain.

When the Lord said to Abraham, "Go from your country, your people and your father's household to the land I will show you," God wasn't just telling Abraham to resettle in another country. At least, that's not what the first audience, the Hebrews, understood it to be about. Not ultimately. The Hebrews saw this call from God to Abraham as more than just about geography; it was far more about *identity*. The journey that God was inviting Abraham into was an existential journey far more than it was a geographical one.[13]

Here's how we know that something else is going on with this invitation Abraham received. The Hebrew word God used here that translates into English "Go" is this powerful and mysterious word *Lech-Lecha*. And this word is less about an outward journey than it is about an *inward* one, because *Lech-Lecha* means: Journey (Lech) to yourself (Lecha). Literally, it means betake yourself, and the Jewish Midrash interprets this to mean, "Go forth to find your authentic self, to learn who you are meant to be."[14]

God says to Abraham, *Lech-Lecha*.

Go.
Journey to yourself.
Learn who you are meant to be.
Follow me where I am leading you, and I will show you the real you inside of you.[15]

In this moment, when God called Abraham to "go," this was not just a command to leave home; it was an invitation to adventure, wonder, and

---

13 For my Bible nerds, yes, there is clearly an actual geographic component to Abraham's story and promise. But the premise of this book is ultimately about the *story-under-the-story*.

14 As with many phrases in the Torah, "*lech lecha*" is enigmatic and open to many interpretations. There is the understanding of *lech lecha* as "Go to yourself," an internal odyssey. It has also been translated as, "Get you out, Go for yourself, Go forth, Go out." That is to say, disassociate from where you are; a call with an external echo to it. In other words, this phrase is a mystery. But what is clear is that lech lecha involves more than a geographical move.

15 I hope that the real me inside of me has the physique of Thor. My wife also hopes this.

self-discovery. *Lech-Lecha* is about starting a new chapter and confronting the very assumptions by which we live.

Are you tracking?

Because when you understand what *Lech-Lecha* is saying, then everything else that follows begin to become clear and fall into place.

If you have been in church for a while, this is likely a new version of the Abrahamic story. I was always sort of taught that Abraham's story was about *arriving* in a land, when it was actually first a story about the *transformation* of a life. We miss the soul of the story of Abraham's call when we turn the story of Abraham into a story of a man who did the right things; in all actuality, the story is really about Abraham becoming the right person. The story of Abraham is a story of *becoming* far more than it is a story of *doing*. The outward journey of Abraham really is but a metaphor for the even more important inward journey that Abraham was being invited to take.

Lech-Lecha.

Go to yourself, and I will show you, *you.*

Dag Hammarskjold said, "The longest journey is the journey inwards." This was the long journey that Abraham was being invited to take. When God said, "Go to the land which I will show you" could also be read, "to the land where I will show you." So, the idea here is that it is not that God just showed Abraham the land but that God was about to take Abraham to the place where God could show and reveal Abraham's truest self. God was showing Abraham, Abraham.

Lech-Lecha was a call to venture into the unknown that will culminate with God showing us who we really are. But in order to get to that place, we will need to be ready to leave behind everything we thought we knew about ourselves and everything we thought we knew about how life works. And when you do, the result of that journey will be that God shows you, you.

Jewish history begins with an invitation to go to yourself because, as Rabbi Schneur Zalman of Liadi said, "There, in the land, God will show you your essence."

That is what God is inviting Abraham into, and perhaps this is why we all need Abraham's story—because that is what God is calling all of us into. Perhaps the reason that this story has resonated with billions of people throughout human history is because Abraham reminds us about the human journey that we all must take if we are going to follow where life is calling us.

Because prior to being called by God, Abraham was not a notable man. We have no reason to believe that Abraham had some sort of spectacular credentials that would make him the obvious candidate for this sort of invitation. As a matter of fact, the Torah does not even call him an *ish tzaddik*, "a righteous man," as it does for Noah. Abraham had not yet accomplished anything of major significance, and he had no real notoriety. But what he did have was courage and the willingness to follow life when it called and invited him to journey inward and find his truest self. He was brave enough to embark on the long journey inward and learn who he could become.

And this is good news for you and me because you might think that you're
Just a student,
Just a mom,
Just an engineer,
Just a lawyer,
Just a teacher,
Just an average person.

Just a _____.

But the story of Abraham reminds us that, if you don't have much in the way of fame, you are the perfect candidate for a move of God. When you read throughout the Hebrew and Christian Scriptures, you can't help but get this sense that the God found in those pages is a God of the underdog. God is the God of the outcast and the ignored, and this God is constantly remembering the forgotten. Not only that, there is no indication that Abraham was looking for God. But it is clear that God was looking for Abraham. That is why the call of *Lech-Lecha* matters—because it is the story of all of us, and it is a call for all of us

To embark on the journey inward,
to leave behind the pain of the past,
to break away from the familiar,
to leave behind all the things that make you a carbon copy of someone else and to embrace the unknown.[16]

And you may not have been looking for God, but God has been looking for *you*.

This story is a glimpse into what the future holds for you if you decide to follow where life is calling you. If we follow in the footsteps of Abraham and embark on our long journey inward that we too will discover who we truly are. Because it is when you take this journey that God shows you, you.

Over the past few years, I have seen the word "deconstructed" used more and more. The idea of deconstruction is that you are letting go of and unraveling yourself from unhelpful, unhealthy, or unsubstantiated values, doctrines, systems, or teachings regarding God, the Bible, the church, and what it means to be human.[17] It has been a shame to see so many churches,

---

16   All I can think of is the song "Into The Unknown" from the Frozen 2 soundtrack. And now that is twice I have referenced music from Frozen. I regret nothing.

17   This was probably too simple of a definition. I also read "deconstruction" defined this way: "It's examining your faith from the inside looking for potential weaknesses. The analogy I like to use is, before you set sail on a cruise ship, you'll see it in harbour

friends, and parents condemn a person who is going through a deconstruction of faith.

One time Jesus taught about how we shouldn't put new wine in old wineskins. Why? Because the old wineskins wouldn't be able to handle the new wine without bursting open. If that isn't a metaphor for how growth works, then I don't know what is. Is it possible that the tension you feel in your faith is because God is trying to pour something new into your life, and you're still trying to contain it in an old wineskin?

Because in order to learn something new, we often must unlearn or let go of something *old*.

Before we could learn that the world was round, we had to unlearn that the earth was flat. As a white man who desires to learn how to be an antiracist, I first have had to unlearn the doctrines of white supremacy that has informed my life as a white American male. I've discovered that, if you say that you want to learn but refuse to unlearn, then you don't really want to learn. The day you stop learning is the day you become a fundamentalist, and don't be fooled by the name; fundamentalism isn't very fun.[18]

After all, what is fun about having a worldview so small that it has no room for new ideas or evolution of thought?

I think you could make the case that Abraham was the first person to go through deconstruction. He lived in a polytheistic world, and tradition holds that his own father not only was a polytheist but owned a shop that sold idols of various gods for worship. I think many of us assume that Abraham

---

and people applying a fresh coat of paint, sealing up any gaps and dealing with the rust. This is done so it doesn't sink once you get out to sea. And that's essentially the same thing that we're saying about faith. It's about taking ownership over what you believe and potentially letting go of some of the things that no longer work."–John Williamson

18 Ew, that was such a Dad joke.

was always this monotheistic follower of God who held all the same beliefs we do about God, faith, and spirituality. But the journey of Abraham is a journey of deconstruction. It's a journey of Abraham unlearning what he had always thought to be true about how God worked and behaved.

I mean, do you remember that one story about God telling Abraham to kill his only son?

And do you remember how Abraham was actually going to comply?

Have you ever read that story and thought, *Why in the world would Abraham do that*? Sure, if you are a parent, there might be moments that you want to metaphorically "kill your kids," but you would never actually do it. If you haven't thought that to yourself while reading the story of Abraham almost sacrificing his son Isaac, then you have not read the story very honestly.

So what gives?

Why would Abraham even consider doing such a thing?

Because sacrificing your child was something Abraham had learned is what the gods often ask of you. That is just how the gods behaved in the world of Abraham.

Abraham went along with it because that's what he had always learned to be true about the gods.

Abraham was still deconstructing.

So why does God ask Abraham to sacrifice his only son, Isaac? Is the God of Abraham just like all the other gods he had learned about?

No. And that is sort of the point of the story.

God intervenes before Abraham kills his son Isaac and stops the sacrifice from happening. Why? Because God was helping Abraham learn what God was actually like by confronting and helping Abraham *unlearn* what he had always thought God was like. God was walking Abraham through his deconstruction and providing Abraham new material to begin his reconstruction. *Lech-Lecha* was not only an invitation for Abraham to engage in a journey of deconstruction of self and God but also a promise that, in the end, Abraham would experience a *reconstruction* of self and a *revelation* about God. You need both deconstruction and reconstruction, and that is what the journey of *Lech-Lecha* is about.[19]

So if you have sensed that you are in the middle of a chapter of deconstruction in your life, you are in good company. If you find yourself in a space of unlearning, then you are in good company. And Abraham's story is hope for all of us—when we feel the ground of everything we thought was true begin to shake beneath us, it is because life is beckoning us to journey toward a new land of knowledge and depth and meaning. Tension is just a sign that you are being stretched. So if you feel tension in your faith, perhaps it is because God is making room in the wineskin of your soul to pour in some new wine.

Lech-Lecha is a promise that on the other side of our deconstruction journey is a reconstructed version of yourself that God has always seen and wants you to see for yourself. Through your deconstruction, God desires to show you, *you*.

God tells Abraham, *Lech-Lecha*—go to yourself. God invited Abraham into a divine deconstruction project, and Abraham followed. Hopefully, we will, too.

---

19 Richard Rohr calls this journey "The Three Boxes." It goes like this: Order > Disorder > Reorder. And although it is difficult, it is crucial to get to the third box–Reorder. Once we can learn to live in this spacious third place, neither fighting nor fleeing reality but holding the creative tension itself, we are in the spacious place of grace out of which all newness comes.

In this moment, even the bed,
Its sheets skimming the floor, collecting dust
In the sunlight, appears to be gilded
And the kitchen sink that holds last night's dishes,
May resemble a cradle; because there is life inside.
And it is the same way with children who, in play
Roll like worms in the dirt and say
They are really flowers.
See how they stand,
As we all do, on holy ground
That at first looks like mud.
When, after a dream of death, we rise up, alive
Ready to walk into the dark
Unknown of the day, each step a whisper
Of lech lecha.
—Magin LaSov Gregg

Chapter 3

The Danger of Safety

"The history of God's people is not a record of God searching for courageous men and women who could handle the task, but God transforming the hearts of cowards and empowering them to live courageous lives."—Unknown

"Some people are so afraid of failing they stop dreaming; others are so afraid of dreaming they start failing."—Bob Goff

And so our journey with Abraham begins.

Well, sort of. Because before we can talk anymore about Abraham, we need to talk about his father, Terah.

Terah's life is only given a few lines in the entirety of the Hebrew Scriptures, but it serves as a haunting and cautionary tale to those who wish to respond when life calls. Because before we are introduced to Abraham, the one who heard and responded to life when it called, the Hebrew story introduces us to Abraham's father, Terah...

Who also heard a call and also responded.

But for some unknown reason, he broke down on the border of his destiny.

We're not told much about Terah. Much of his life is shrouded in mystery and speculation. But Genesis 11 tells us enough about Terah to warrant a pause.

Genesis 11:31–32 says: "One day Terah took his son Abraham, his daughter-in-law Sarai (his son Abraham's wife), and his grandson Lot (his son Haran's child) and moved away from Ur of the Chaldeans. He was headed for the land of Canaan, but they stopped at Haran and settled there. Terah lived for 205 years and died while still in Haran."

This is pretty much all that the Hebrew Scriptures tell us about Abraham's father, Terah. He was a single dad who one day took his two sons, Abraham and Haran, along with Abraham's wife, Sarai, and grandson, Lot, and moved from their home in Ur with the plans of making a new home in Canaan. But something happened, because they stopped in a city called Haran, settled there, and we're told that, after 205 years on this earth, Terah died while still in Haran.

Riveting stuff. I think we have an Oscar winning movie script on our hands.[20]

Okay, maybe not, but it is interesting. Or at least, it should be interesting, but it's probably not, because a story about a person moving from one city to another isn't that exciting; it isn't that revolutionary,—at least not to our twenty-first-century minds.

Because we live in a nomadic culture, don't we?

How many people do you know that stay in the same city or town for the entirety of their lives? Although some people do stay in one place their whole lives, those people are becoming increasingly rare to find.

Over the past eight years of pastoring in San Francisco, it has at times felt like I am pastoring a parade because most people pass through San Francisco instead of moving to San Francisco in order to plant roots. Most people are here for a few years and then they move. Every time a friend of mine asks

---

20 It would at least be a better movie than the movie "Green Lantern."

me to meet them up for coffee, I know that "the talk" is coming. The talk where they tell me they are leaving San Francisco, and I pretend to be happy for them. If you have ever lived in a city like San Francisco, you know what I'm talking about. But the truth is that, with the advent of the internet, social media, working remotely, and technology like FaceTime, it's easier than ever to uproot your life and explore the world. And that's why, likely to you, this story of Terah uprooting his family and moving to a new city is not that compelling or shocking.

But in Terah's day, around 2056 BCE, this was *not* normal.

Not only did he not have the advantages of FaceTime or Facebook, but to pack up your life and move your family would almost certainly effect you socially, economically, and vocationally. This sort of move was not normal. It would be the sort of thing that your family would hold an intervention over.[21] So, before we move forward, the fact that Terah left his home, his people, and his livelihood gives us plenty of reasons to safely assume that something must have majorly disrupted Terah's life.

So much so that he couldn't stay where he was any longer.

So much so that he was willing to put his own fortune, family, and future on the line in order to get out of town and start life somewhere new.

Because of this, we should ask some questions about Terah and, by extension, some questions about ourselves. The story of Terah should cause us to ask questions like the following:

What is it that caused Terah to decide to leave everything he had known and move to a faraway place called Canaan?

---

21 Which reminds me of the episode on The Office where Michael holds an intervention for Meredith after she set her hair on fire after drinking too much. Classic.

Abraham, the son of Terah, will later hear the voice of God and decide to leave Haran and go to Canaan. Was the voice Abraham heard that told him to go to Canaan the *same one* that Terah also heard that prompted him to move to Canaan?

Because of this, some believe that God originally called Terah to go to Canaan *before* God called Abraham. So was Abraham's call the result of Terah not finishing his?

Now lean in and stay with me. This is where it gets interesting.

We're told that Terah settled in Haran and never reached Canaan. So is it possible that, if Terah had traveled to Canaan our Bibles would refer to God as the God of Terah instead of referring to God as the God of Abraham?

If Terah hadn't settled in Haran, would Terah have been known as the Father of the Jews, instead of Abraham?

If Terah hadn't settled, would he, instead of Abraham, be the forefather of Judaism, Islam, and Christianity?

If Terah had made it to Canaan, would kids in churches be singing an annoyingly memorable song about how "Father Terah had many sons, and many sons have Father Terah?"

And the questions don't end there because now I am forced to ask the following:

Did Terah miss out on his legacy because he settled too soon?

Could this be why the author of Genesis curiously felt that, with the little bit of Terah's story we were given, he needed to remind us *three times* that Terah didn't get to where he had originally set out to go? Why the repetition?

Is it possible that this story is included in the Scriptures because it is about more than just a man named Terah?

Is it possible that we have this brief history of Terah not so that we can know who Terah was but so we could know who Terah never *became*?

Is Terah's life a cautionary tale? Does his short story serve as a warning to anyone who is thinking about stopping too soon?

Which leads to an even more important series of questions for you now:

Has life been calling you forward?

Is there any part of you that is settling too soon instead of advancing?

If so, why?

Is it possible that someone else is celebrating a victory that was meant for me, but I missed because I stopped too soon?

If Terah's life was written down and remembered for us as a warning about what happens when you stop too soon, then what could you miss out on if you stopped moving forward and into where life is calling you?

We all know that leaving everything you know to follow life when it calls is certainly a risk.

But does Terah's life warn us that playing it safe is actually the most *dangerous* thing you could ever do with your life?

Chapter 4

Judo Chops and Banana Tubes

"Don't rely too much on labels, for too often they are fables."
—Charles H. Spurgeon

*"To learn who I am, I've had to learn who I am not. You are
not what others think about you. You are not your past. You
are not what you did. You are who God says you are."—Craig
Groeschell*

I recently read about how, in Ancient Rome, if your mother was a slave,
you were automatically a slave. The term they used for someone born into
slavery was *vernae* (var-n-eye), which is plural, and *verna*, which is singular.
And these Roman vernae would sometimes have to wear a slave collar just
in case they ran away. Think about the collar you might have your dog
wear, except far more inhumane and far more barbaric. One actual Roman
vernae collar said this:

*"I am Asellus, slave of Praeiectus, who is an administrative officer in the
Department of the Grain Supply. I have escaped from my post. Capture me,
for I have run away. Return me to the barber's shop near the Temple of Flora."*

Essentially, these Roman slaves would be branded from birth, literally carrying around their neck the word "slave" and the identity that comes along
with it.

Can you imagine having that sort of identity not only hanging on your neck but, even worse, your soul?

My dog Riggins wears a collar around his neck with his name on it and our phone number. Why? Because, if he were to ever be lost, I would be sobbing and in the fetal position for weeks. I love that little ball of fur even though he is a cat in a dog's body. But that collar he wears exists to protect him from harm. These Roman collars weren't the result of love and protection. I think Roman slaveholders wanted their slaves to see and be reminded every day of what Rome thought of them. They were slaves. Nothing more and nothing less. I think Roman slaveholders understood that the greatest slavery wasn't the collar wrapped around their neck; it was the false identity that wrapped around their hearts.

Which brings me to Terah.

Terah may not have been born into slavery, and he wasn't branded with a Roman collar. But in the ancient world of the Bible, names were a big deal. Your name was not simply a title that people would call you as much as it was seen as a sort of prophecy about your life. It wasn't just what you would use to reserve a table at a restaurant or what would be on your driver's license. When parents in the ancient world picked your name, they would do so with great intentionality because, very much unlike today, names weren't seen as titles; they were seen as destinies. Your name had the power to become your biography before you even finished your life.

I think we still, in a sense, understand that a name has a lot of power. I think about one of my favorite actors, Joaquin Bottom. Of course you don't know him as that; you know him as Joaquin Phoenix. Or one of my favorite movies is Django Unchained starring Eric Bishop, also known as, Jamie Foxx. Why did these actors, along with many others in the entertainment industry, change their names? Because, whether you agree or not, the belief is that the wrong name can keep you from your preferred future.

There is also the other side of the spectrum, where children are given names with little to no thought at all. I had a friend in high school whose last name was Time. So his parents gave him the first name Justin. So his name was Justin Time. If you don't understand why that is funny, just say his full name slowly until it sinks in. The irony about Justin Time is that he was perpetually *late* for everything. Or I recall another friend whose last name was Tagad (pronounced: Tuh-God); we joked about naming his first child, Honest. Honest Tagad. So that every time he yelled at her, he would say "Honest Tagad!" We thought it was funny. I wonder if he went through with it.

My wife's name is Jena, and Jena means "little bird." So cute. Just like my wife. It's perfect. Well done to my in-laws.

My name is Travis. What does Travis mean? It means "toll gate."

Thanks, Mom and Dad. You had a plethora of names to give me, and you chose, "toll gate."

The point is, today we simply don't think about names like they did in the ancient world. Because in the ancient world of the Bible, names really mattered. I think of the story of Isaac's son, who they named Jacob. Jacob means "heel grabber," which is a euphemism for a liar and a cheat. And his biography turns out to be just that—a story of one deception after another. That is until Jacob has a cage fight with an angel in the middle of the night; channeling Conor McGregor, Jacob says to the angel, "I will not let you go unless you bless me." Then the angel does something that changed Jacob's life forever.[22]

He didn't undo Jacob's mistakes.
He didn't erase Jacob's failures.

---

22 I like to imagine Jacob with an Irish accent like McGregor. It adds a lot to the story.

He didn't change Jacob's past.
He gave Jacob a *new name*.
He gave Jacob a new identity.

And in a single moment, it was like the glass ceiling to his future had been shattered. We see this name change happen to many people in the Scriptures, like when Abram's name was changed to Abraham and Simon's name was changed to Peter. Changing a person's name was sort of God's thing.

Why though?

Because names carried such weight that the wrong name would be like a collar around your neck, keeping you from ever rising above the identity that someone else gave you. So, if God wanted to change someone's destiny, he would need to change their identity, and if he were to change someone's identity, God would often need to change their name. And this is because God knows something that we forget in our image-obsessed world that tries to convince you that you would be a more satisfied and happier human if you were just prettier, thinner, wealthier, or more popular. And what God knows is that, if you really want to see the world around you changed, it begins with changing the world *within* you. When God invites someone in the Scriptures to travel into something new, he first uproots false identities that you have come into agreement with.

When God gives someone a new name, it is because he is inviting them into a new future.

And all of this name talk brings us back to Abraham's father, Terah.

Because one of the first things I'll do when I try and understand a character in the Scriptures is I will take a look at their name and, most importantly, the meaning of the name. I want to know what identity they were born into. I want to know what inner material they are working with because it often sheds light on why a person does what they do in the Bible.

And Terah proves this theory to be true because the name Terah means "delay" or "wanderer."

Delay.

Wanderer.

If you haven't forgotten the brief biography of Terah that we received in Genesis 12, delay and wander were exactly what Terah did until eventually he died in Haran. The more I get to know the story of Terah, the more I begin to empathize with him, and his humanity begins to show. Because I wonder if Terah left his homeland in Ur as an act of rebellion against the name and ultimately the identity he had been given since his birth. I wonder if, every time Terah didn't finish a task or wasn't assertive enough, that those around him would roll their eyes and say, "Oh, well. That's Terah for you." Maybe everyone around Terah doubted that the man known as "delay" would ever do or finish anything with his life. I wonder if perhaps the man named "wanderer" always felt that life and joy eluded him, and so the wanderer wandered toward Canaan, hoping to find what he was looking for. I'm not sure. We're not provided a full glimpse into Terah's life. But the little we do know seems to indicate that, in the end, Terah never outgrew his name. In the end, the man named "delay" and "wanderer" lived up to the identity that he was given.

Or maybe it's more accurate to say that Terah lived *down* to the identity that he was given.

Instead of being known as the man who listened and followed when life called and went to Canaan, he is known as the man who delayed and wandered and did so until eventually he died in Haran.

Instead of being known for arriving in Canaan, he is known for how he wandered and never got where he intended to go.

Which, of course, is what happens to all of us when we come into agreement with the wrong identity over our lives: it ends up becoming a sort of collar that is always calling us back to our place of slavery. When we live with the wrong identity, it is like the app on your phone that is not compatible with the operating system and shuts down any time you try and open it. When you try to build a life that is incompatible with your operating system, then your efforts are eventually shut down, and the life you hope for never really opens up for you.

I was challenged by this question from author Carlos Whittaker in his book *How to Kill a Spider*. He asked, "What lies have you come into agreement with in your life?" Which I would argue is not just a question, it is *the* question that we must answer if we are going to step into a new future. This is where religion lets so many of us down. Because in far too many churches we are told that the human problem is a *behavior* problem. So we're often taught implicitly (sometimes explicitly) that the most important thing about our lives is sinning less. Do less bad things and replace them with more good things and God will be happy with you. But I can't tell you how many people I know that followed this theology right off the cliff into disappointment.

They did the right things.
They prayed the prayers.
They gave to those in need.
They managed their behavior the best they knew how.

And yet they still felt like slaves to something deeper that would not let them be fully free.

I think this is because at the core of the human dilemma is not a behavior problem but a *believing* problem, and what God wants to do in a person's life is less about changing behaviors and more about changing beliefs— especially what you believe about yourself and what you believe God sees when he looks at you. Because God knows that who you believe you are, that internal world you live in, is the material you're working with to build your life. Perhaps this is a part of what Jesus meant when he told us that no one can build a house made on sand. We're all using material to build our lives; the question is, is it the sort of material that can actually build a life worth living? If not, the problem is likely not found in your behavior but in your *beliefs*.

What lies have you come into agreement with in your life?

What beliefs are you holding onto?

Or maybe it's more accurate to say what beliefs are holding onto *you*?

I remember one time when I was a kid, my family and I were visiting my aunt and uncle in Austin, Texas. I loved visiting them because—let me be honest—they were rich. They were like have-their-initials-etched-on-the-bottom-of-their-swimming-pool rich. So when we visited them, I knew that we were going to have some fun. I remember, this particular summer in Austin because, we went to my aunt and uncle's lake house, and we spent days swimming, riding jet skis, and cruising around in my uncle's boat. Like I said, *rich*. Also, the lake's name was Lake Travis, so in my head, it was *my* lake. I was king of Lake Travis. During this summer at Lake Travis, my uncle got a new toy for all of us to enjoy—a banana tube.

If you don't know what a banana tube is, it's an inflatable tube that a few people can all ride at the same time as a boat pulls you around the lake at Millennium Falcon speeds. I remember my first ride on the banana tube because I was riding in the very front with my two older sisters behind me. We were flying down the lake. I was afraid that I might have made my uncle angry because it became quickly apparent that he was in fact trying to kill us. So I was holding on for dear life, white knuckling the entire ride, refusing to let go and skip across the lake like a human-sized pebble. And things were going well until we hit a wave in the lake and it shot the tube into the air. Somehow, I was able to maintain my ninja-like grip on the handles of the banana tube.

But my sister behind me was not so lucky.

I turned around, and I saw my sister was holding onto the handles of the banana tube, but when we'd hit that bump, it had thrown her off of her seat. So she was holding onto her handles, but her body was hanging on the side of the tube, skipping across the water. I'll never forget, as my sister looked at me with fear in her eyes, she cried out, swallowing lake water in-between each word, "Travis! (Gurgle) Please...help...(gurgle, gurgle) me!"

Then she slowly reached out her hand toward mine so that I could grab her and pull her back onboard the banana tube. It was like a scene from a movie where a person extends their hand in one final attempt to avoid demise. I could hear the music building behind me. So I began to extend my hand toward her.

But then...

I remembered how it seemed that my sister had made it her life goal to torture me relentlessly. From name-calling, making me be her "servant for the day" so that I could have use of the TV remote control, and sending her boyfriend to beat me up. And I realized that, if I'd tried bring her back onboard the banana tube, I would have been pulled into the depths of the Lake Travis right along with her, and that would be the end of my ride on the banana tube. So I did what any good little brother would do if he were in my position.

I put her out of her misery and judo-chopped her one remaining wrist.

Rumor has it that her body is still skipping down Lake Travis to this very day.

Now, this story might be, and probably is, a lesson on how to be a terrible brother. But it also just might be a good visual for what it's going to look like for you to be free to move forward in your life. Because so many people have false identities that have been torturing them relentlessly and keeping them from being free. And if you try to save those false identities and hold onto them, it will take you down with it. And so you have the choice every day whether you will hold onto what will certainly bring you down or judo chop that thing and be free to enjoy the rest of this ride called "life."

I know that is likely an oversimplification. But the point here is that you have the choice to be free. You have the ability to choose what gets on board your heart and what doesn't. And what we allow to stay onboard our heart will determine the outcome of our life. Like the Proverbs say, "Guard your heart, for it determines the course of your life" (Proverbs 4:23). We'll talk more about this in a few chapters.

Terah's life is a sobering warning for all of us about the power that our most deeply held identities and beliefs have over our lives. The short biography of Terah's life is but a cautionary reminder that, in this one life you have been given, you will either *define* or *be defined*. You will either let yourself become a product of the intention of others or you will decide to become the product of living an intentional life. For some of you, before you can follow where life is calling you into, you will need to break some agreements with lies, you will need to cut some collars that you've been wearing, and you will need to judo chop some identities that are holding onto your heart and have been keeping you from living into your fullest and truest God-given identity.

Terah reminds us that, before you can engage the full life that is awaiting you, you will need to cut ties with the false identities that are beneath you. Because what awaits you on the other side of those lies is a fuller life as you become your truest self.

Chapter 5

Nakusa

"Living our lives based on the opinions of others will only cause us to lose our souls and our way."—Unknown

"God's never looked in your mirror and wished He saw someone else."—Bob Goff

Terah's name shaped his identity, and his identity shaped his future. Terah is no exception because this is how it works for all of us. The identity we hold is the material we build our futures with.

If you could sum up the identity that you hold about yourself in a single word, I wonder what it would be? Your most honest answer to that question is the material that you are building your life with. Is it the kind of material that will build the life you were created to live? Are you living up to an identity or, like Terah, do you find yourself living *down* to your identity?

This reminds me of a story I once read about how there are many girls in India named Nakusa.

Nakusa means "unwanted."

This was happening because families with little property or land wanted it to remain in their name and, as a result, preferred to have sons who they could pass their wealth down to. The origin of this practice of naming their daughters Nakusa was born out of a superstition that, by doing this, they could ensure that their next child was a boy. It was a way of telling the gods that they did not want another girl. And a boy that is born after several girls is often named after a god as a way of thanking the gods for providing a son they've truly wanted.

Sadly, but not surprisingly, nearly seventy percent of Nakusas surveyed faced some sort of humiliation on account of their name. Many Nakusas did not even realize what their name meant until later in their lives, when others would begin to taunt them because of their name.

Nakusa.

Unwanted.

Names and labels have this way of shaping our truest beliefs about ourselves, don't they? And if every human being was created to create, then it is our truest beliefs about ourselves that we use as the brick and mortar that we use to build our future. We are always building the world around us from the material within us.

To put it most simply, you are always building what you believe.

Think about it. Have you ever heard the phrase "Hurting people hurt people?" It's true in a lot of ways, isn't it? I recently watched a series on Netflix called *I Am A Killer*. You know, just another light and happy television show that you watch before peacefully going to sleep. The premise: they would interview Death Row inmates so that we could know their stories and understand their humanity.

And do you know what I realized?

Not one single person was born a killer, but at some point in their lives, a killer was birthed in them.

They had birthdays, played with toys, went on dates, and did all the things that every one of us has done. But the difference was that each of them had an encounter or a series of encounters that wounded them so deeply that the content of their lives was being informed in the context of their wounds. And the truth is that all of us carry wounds and it is what we do with our wounds that often define what we do with our lives. Some turn their greatest wounds into their greatest victories, while others turn their greatest wounds into great violence.

The context of our wounds has a way of informing the content of our lives without us even really knowing it.

I wonder, if you were to identify your wound with a single word, what that word would be? Maybe your word for your wound would be words like worthless, abused, mistake, failure, divorced, abortion, racism, or abandoned. For so many people, their word has stuck with them and has become the material of their identity. Isn't it interesting how a single word can continue to echo throughout the rest of our lives and inform the lives we build?

Now, the Hebrew people took this whole words-are-powerful thing even further.

They actually believed that words have the capacity to *create*. There is no greater example of this belief then when the author of Genesis recounts how the world came into existence.[23] And how did it all begin? How did creation come into existence? What was the material God used to begin building the cosmos?

---

23 Many Christians have advocated reading the creation poem in Genesis chapters 1-2 as history, I am not sure that's the story's intention. I don't know if the point that the author is trying to drive home in Genesis is that God can create the world in seven literal days. As you peel back the story and compare it to other ancient creation stories, you begin to see more going on here. Genesis is less historical than it is poetic, and like all good poetry, there is always a bigger truth underneath each line that the poet is trying to get us to understand.

God *spoke.*

And because of this, the Hebrews have held onto this idea that God's words create *worlds.*

And words still create worlds, don't they?

Have you ever had someone say something to you, but there was that one word or one statement they said that you couldn't get out of your head? You can't even remember the majority of the conversation, but you remember that one thing they said. So you lay in bed all night thinking about it and processing it, and then you start drawing conclusions about what they meant by what they said, and before you know it, you have created an entire story around what that person meant by what they said. Now, have you ever done this only to find out that it was a misunderstanding and that your conclusions about what they said were wrong, and then you feel a little silly because you allowed yourself to go to a pretty dark place over a single word?

Have you ever asked, "Why do I do that to myself?"

It's a good question.

Why *do* we do this to ourselves?

Why do words have the ability to take us down roads that we never would have thought we'd go down? We do this because words create worlds. A single word has the capacity to create a world of wonder or a world of chaos within our souls.

Have you ever said something so hurtful to someone and you knew it just by the look on their face and, in that moment, you realized that your words did something very real to that person?

I'll never forget Labor Day weekend in 2017, when Jena and I were about to go surfing. And by surfing, I really mean falling. We aren't very good. My surfer friends would call me a "kook." Which is just a funny word for a rookie surfer. Anyways, I packed up our surfboards, towels, and wetsuits, and I strapped everything to the roof of our car then drove the hour and thirty minutes to get to Santa Cruz. Finally, when we arrived, we went to check how the waves looked. It looked like it was going to be a solid day, and just before we were going to walk back to the car to get our boards, Jena looked at me, took a deep breath, and said, "Travis, I won't be able to go surfing today."

Honestly, I was kind of annoyed because I had just packed up all our stuff and drove all the way to the beach, and she was just now deciding to tell me that she wasn't planning on surfing? But then she explained why...

"I'm not going to be able to surf...because I'm pregnant."

Pregnant.

I'm not sure what my face looked like when she told me this, but I know that this word dropped on me like an anvil, and at that moment, I began to see multiple pictures of Jena's face circling mine like a Saturday morning cartoon. That single word reverberated through my soul, and I've never been the same since in the best sort of way. In that single moment, that word opened up a new world for me. This new world was created by that single word—pregnant.

But not all words are created equal, though, are they? Some words can create a world of hope, while others create a world of heartache. For example, when my dad sat me down in my bedroom when I was in Junior High and told me that he was leaving and moving to Kentucky with his wife and their kids and then he told me that I couldn't come with him.

Leaving.

Moving.

You can't go.

For years, these words were stuck on my soul like a bad tattoo, and as much as I tried to rub or scratch them off, they were there to stay. There is no laser removal for the words that tattoo themselves to your soul. And when my dad finished telling me that he was moving and that I couldn't go, it created a world in me, and this world was called "unloved," and it was a world that only I was the resident of.

Or I think of when my mom gave birth to twins. I was too young to fully understand what was going on, but I have a vague memory of walking into my mom's room and seeing her sweating and in pain, and I had gone in there to bring her a teddy bear, hoping to make her feel better. But little did I know that my mom was about to experience a tragedy that would create a world within her that, for the rest of her life, would be impossible to shake. Because my mom would soon get the word from the doctor that both of her babies had died shortly after birth.

Death.

Understandably, this word created a world of heartbreak for my mom, and in many ways the context of that wound would begin to inform much of the content of her life.

So, I wonder, are there any words you are living with? I wonder if there are any wounds you are carrying within you that are creating a world around you. I've been told that 'time heals all wounds'; I don't know about you, but I have found that to not be entirely true. Time doesn't heal all wounds; God does[24]. But I have found that God doesn't just zap our wounds away. We have a role to play in our journey of healing from the wounds that are

24 And a good therapist helps too.

informing our lives. Although we cannot heal our wounds, our job is to reveal our wounds. Because you won't heal from what you are unwilling to reveal.

This is why I am a huge advocate of therapy. Why? Because it creates a space for us to drag our skeletons out of the closet and expose them. There is something about being honest about our wounds that empties our wounds of their power over us. Which, of course, means the opposite is true, and that is that silence and isolation only make our wounds grow that much stronger. If you want to heal it, you need to reveal it. Our role is to make eye contact with our wounds and reveal them, and as we do that, God begins to stitch us up and put us back together.

Are there any wounds that you need to make eye contact with today?

Any words that you need to reveal?

If you have opted for isolation and silence, may I ask, how is that working out for you?

We were told that sticks and stones may break our bones but words will never hurt us. Which is total crap, isn't it?

Because the right word can create a world of possibility, while the wrong word can create another reality that is a darker reality that you feel trapped in—like the Upside Down from *Stranger Things*.

I wonder if this is why God, throughout the Scriptures, often gave people new names—because the right word has the ability to turn your world that was once upside-down right-side up. It's like God knows that the wounds we carry, if they aren't transformed, will be *transferred* into the future we create.

If our hurt isn't transformed, it will be transferred.
If the abuse isn't transformed, it will be transferred.
If our anger isn't transformed, it will be transferred.

And far too often we only allow God to treat our symptoms, when God really wants to heal the source of our greatest sickness. Instead, far too many of us put band aids on bullet wounds.

One of my favorite stories in the Christian Scriptures is the story of Jesus raising a man named Lazarus back to life in John 11. Lazarus had been dead for a few days, and it appeared to everyone there that Jesus was too late to do anything. They had requested that Jesus show up. They needed Jesus to show up. But Jesus waited, and by the time he showed up, not only was Lazarus dead but he was already wrapped up and in his tomb. It is the sort of story that, when read honestly, can mess with your view of Jesus a little bit.

Have you ever felt like God was just too late?

Have you needed God to show up and he didn't?

What's so powerful about this story is that, once Jesus finally arrived at the funeral, Jesus told Mary and Martha to let him go into the tomb of Lazarus. But they both told Jesus that he shouldn't do that, and the reason was because Lazarus had been in the tombs for a few days; they said it would smell terrible. The King James Version actually says that Martha told Jesus he couldn't go into the tomb because "he stinketh." Is that not the best Bible verse ever?

"He stinketh."[25] [26]

But Jesus didn't care, and he ordered the stone to be rolled away, and Jesus entered into the tomb and did not appear to care how bad Lazarus would stinketh. Because he then proceeded to raise Lazarus from the dead to the amazement of the crowd watching.

---

25 John 11:39, King James Version
26 I still think this would be a great tattoo.

This story means so much to me because it tells me something about God: God is not scared of the areas of my life that "stinketh." He knows the parts of my heart that reek of anger, pain, and betrayal. And if Jesus is like God, that means God is like Jesus. Which means, when we see that Jesus is willing to enter a tomb that stinketh, we are seeing what God does. Not only that, but this is arguably Jesus's greatest miracle of his earthly ministry (besides, you know, resurrecting himself). This tells me that God does his greatest work in our darkest circumstances.

But here's the catch.

Before Jesus could enter the tomb, they had to roll away the stone.

And the same is true for you.

God is ready to enter into the darkest places of your heart, but you must roll away the stone and let him in to do his work. Because his job is to heal, but your job is to reveal. I believe that vulnerability is perhaps the most courageous human act a person can do. Brené Brown once said, "Courage is telling your story with your whole heart." If you are going to follow life where it calls, you will need to roll away some stones. Your future depends on your courage to tell your story with your whole heart and allow those part of your heart that stinketh to be revealed so that they can be healed.

And this is so important for us to understand because, as I said earlier, the world within us is what we use as the material to create a world around us.

So, I hope you'll allow me to be redundant and ask you one more time: if you were to pause and be most honest with yourself right now and write down the words that you carry, what would they be? And are those words the kind of material you need to create a future worth fighting for, or will they create a future that you will one day try and forget? Is it time to reveal those words and those wounds so that you can begin to be healed and create a new future with mew material?

Let's go back to the story of the Nakusas for a moment.

It actually has a great ending.

An organization held a renaming ceremony where 285 Nakusas were given the opportunity to change their names. These girls chose names of Indian celebrities, goddesses, or more simple terms such as "beautiful." At the end of the ceremony, a couple of the girls were interviewed, and these girls said this about receiving their new names: "I'm a new person. Because tomorrow I won't go into class and be known as Nakusa. Instead of 'unwanted,' I am a new person."[27]

In other words, when they got a new word for their life,
the ceiling was shattered.
The script was rewritten.
A new destiny was birthed.
They now had new material to build their lives with.

What word are you living with? What wounds are you holding onto? Before you can step into where life is calling you to, do you need to hold a renaming ceremony for yourself to reveal the destructive word you've been living with?

The word that you've come into agreement with.
The word that was given to you by someone else.
The word that has been choking life from your soul.

Learn from the Nakusas and learn from Terah. In this life, let me say it again, either you define or you will be defined.

God has some words for you, and I want you to know that these words are the truest words about you. You didn't do anything to earn these words, which means there's nothing you can do to lose them. And if you are willing

---

27 I'm not crying, you're crying.

to reveal the words and wounds that have been informing your life, God will not only heal you but over time replace those old wounds with new words that will become the new material you will build your future with.

Some of these words that God believes about you are...

Loved.
Worthy.
Masterpiece.
Purposeful.
Chosen.
Beautiful.

Just to name a few.

What if today, right now, wherever you are, you held your very own renaming ceremony so that you can start building a life with the right material?

Terah never became his truest self. Sadly, his story is far too common. But I have good news for you today. His story does not need to be yours.

Chapter 6

A Place Called Angry

This is the account of Terah's family. Terah was the father of Abraham, Nahor, and Haran was the father of Lot. But Haran died in Ur of the Chaldeans, the land of his birth, while his father, Terah, was still living. One day Terah took his son Abraham, his daughter-in-law Sarai (his son Abraham's wife), and his grandson Lot (his son Haran's child) and moved away from Ur of the Chaldeans. He was headed for the land of Canaan, but they stopped at Haran and settled there. 32 Terah lived for 205 years and died while still in Haran. —Genesis 11:27–28, 31–32

No one knows exactly why Terah left everything he knew to go to Canaan, and no one knows exactly why he never reached his destination. But we do know something awful happened to Terah that might color in his story a bit for us. Genesis 11 provides a glimpse into what happened:

"But Haran died in Ur of the Chaldeans."

Terah experienced the greatest tragedy that a parent could experience.

His son, his baby boy named Haran, died.

We don't know how he died or even how old he was when he died. But none of that really matters. The author here wants us to know that something absolutely terrible happened to Terah, and it might help us understand why Terah stopped short of where he was intending to go.

Can you even begin to imagine the pain of this loss? Parents aren't supposed to outlive their kids. Parents aren't supposed to bury their kids. But if that wasn't bad enough, some translations actually read like this: "Haran died in the presence of his father Terah."[28] So it is entirely possible that not only did Haran die before his father, but Haran died *before* his father. Meaning Haran died in the presence of his father. Terah witnessed the death of his baby boy with his own eyes. Whether Haran's death was due to disease or a tragic accident we don't know. But what we do know is that Terah experienced a pain so terrible that no parent would ever wish it on even their worst enemy.

Right now I am sitting in a coffee shop, fighting back tears, because all I can think about is my daughter Finley.

I am not sure what I would do if I lost my child. I cannot even begin to imagine the pain and anguish that my wife and I would feel if we were to experience such a tragedy. But I am pretty confident that, if I did go through such a heart-crushing loss, I would want to run away. It would be incredibly tempting to move away and seek some sort of new beginning, somewhere that would get me as far away as possible from anything that reminded me of my pain. As much as I would never want to forget my child, I would quickly do everything I could to get away from the agony of my child's absence.

Do you think this could be why Terah left to go to Canaan?

Is it possible that Terah, in his deep grief for the loss of his son Haran, decided to uproot everything in an attempt to find a fresh start?

What would you do if your own child died before your very eyes?

---

28 Genesis 11:28

We'll never know for sure, but we know that, after the death of Haran, Terah packed up his family and uprooted his entire life in order to set out toward a new land far away called Canaan. But just about halfway there, we're told that Terah stopped on his journey and settled somewhere else.

We are told that Terah settled and he eventually died in a land named

Haran.

The same name as his dead son.

The route from the Ur of the Chaldeans went directly through the town of Haran, which was about halfway between Ur and Canaan. Haran was either a settlement that had been established by Terah's son or a settlement to which at least his name had become attached. As a parent, I don't doubt for a second that coming to the town that bore the name of his dead son caused Terah to be reminded of and relive the pain of his greatest wound. I wonder if it was his pain and loss that derailed his journey? I have to believe that the author of Genesis included this detail in the story for a reason.

Terah set out to a place of hope and a place of healing, but before he could get there, he had to go *through* a place that would remind him of his greatest hurt.

We're told in Genesis 11:31 that they "stopped in Haran and settled there." What is so interesting about this is that, in Hebrew, the word "settled" can also mean "to sit down," and the word Haran, the place, can also be translated as "to be angry." So when Genesis tells us, "He was headed for the land of Canaan, but they stopped at Haran and settled there. Terah lived for 205 years and died while still in Haran," we could also read it to say the following:

Terah was heading for Canaan,
A new place to call home.

A place where he could start over.
A place where he hoped he could heal.
But while on his journey,
Terah stopped in a place called "angry,"
And he sat down.
And he stayed there
until he eventually died.

This story is so human, isn't it?

Because who hasn't tried to start new?

Who hasn't experienced a hurt so deep that they just wanted to run away?

And I bet we all know people who have sat down in a place of hurt, and they stayed there, and it kept them from reaching a place of hope.

I've heard it said before that bitterness causes a person to become a victim twice. First, you are a victim to what had been done to you, and you are a victim a second time because of what you do to yourself. Bitterness, in a lot of ways, is the result of anger that hasn't been grieved yet. When you don't grieve losses and when you don't look at the source of your deepest hurt or anger in the eyes, the result is bitterness. This is why I believe that grief is God's tool for handling life's losses. If you don't grieve, you get stuck. Jesus even once taught this idea when he said, "Blessed are those who mourn."[29]

How could Jesus say that those who mourn are blessed?

I think it's because it is those who love much that will grieve the most. That is the great risk with love—it opens you up to be hurt. And you can try to live a life where you are never hurt, but doing this will require you to live a life where you never love deeply. Have you noticed that it is those in your

---

29 Matthew 5:4

life that you love the most that have hurt you the deepest? That is because great love requires great risk. Love is the source of your greatest joy and happiness, but love will likely also be the source of your greatest pain and heartache. So why is someone blessed when they mourn?

It is because their mourning is a sign that they have loved well.

You mourn what you love, and to live a life of love is a blessed life.

Which would then mean that the opposite is also true: anger is a cursed life.

Maybe you wouldn't use those terms. But it's true, isn't it? I mean, have you ever seen an angry and bitter person who you wanted to model your life after? Of course not. Because anger and bitterness is a life that is stuck on the hamster wheel of pain—as they run through that which is the source of their greatest pain again and again. It's a version of life that can keep you from reaching where life is calling you, because life only calls you one direction, and that is into the future, while anger and bitterness only go one direction, and that's backward into your past.[30]

Every loss clears a space for new opportunities and energies to emerge. So when we don't grieve our losses, we don't clear this space. Ungrieved loss causes us to hold onto hope that we will get back what we lost. Have you ever seen someone experience a breakup anxiously wait for the call or text from their ex? Or the person who is let go of their job and, instead of hunting for their next job, locks himself in his room because he is replaying his loss?

Grieving is about *recognizing* and *releasing*.

You cannot grieve what you don't accept. So grieving loss is first about *recognizing* that you were hurt and let down and that the pain you experienced

---

30 "Bitterness is like drinking poison and waiting for the other person to die."–Joanna Weaver

did, in fact, happen. That abuse was real. That death was real. That hurt or betrayal was real. It's acknowledging its presence in your life. But grieving is also about *releasing*. It's about recognizing its presence in your life but releasing it from having power over your life. It is looking at the reality of your pain and defiantly saying "you will not run my life."

Ungrieved losses begin to inform your life when you allow a past loss to not only have *presence* in your life but also have *power* over your life.

When you're gripping on to something that you lost, your energy and focus are directed to that thing. Until you grieve the loss, you remain bound to the energy of that thing, tied to the past. Grieving frees up your energy, making it available for you to reinvest elsewhere. It frees your hands from their grip on the past so that your arms are open to receive the gifts of the present and future. You will have a difficult time grabbing hold of your future if your hands are already full of your past.

As Setareh Moafi, PhD, once said, "When you allow emotions such as grief to transport you to the depths of your heart, you can hear the lessons of your past, let go, and regain the strength and clarity to more fully experience your authentic self."

You should probably pause to re-read that. It's that important.

I find it so interesting that the biblical author John wrote about a moment when Jesus was overcome with sadness. If you ever went to this place called "Sunday School," this might be the only Bible verse you committed to memory because it's the shortest verse, clocking in at only two words.

John writes it in John 11:35, "Jesus wept."

I have always found it odd that John would include this. After all, most theologians agree that John's agenda in his writings is to make a case for Jesus being God. I don't know about you, but I'm not sure the best way to make a case for Jesus being God is writing how Jesus wept. I think I'd aim for more stories of strength and power and victory, and John includes those stories, but tucked within his gospel document, he also tells us that Jesus weeps too.

Which leads us to a question:

Does God weep?

And why would John want us to know this?

And in this moment, Jesus is weeping over Lazarus, the same guy we had just talked about in the previous chapter. You know, the one Jesus would raise from the dead. So if you are Jesus and you know that you are going to raise Lazarus from the dead...

Then why do you weep?

It's because, before Jesus brings new life, Jesus unapologetically joins people in their heartbreak, loss, and grieves with them.

I've heard this story hundreds of times, and every time, I'm reminded of how God can raise dead things to life. And this is true. But before it was a story of how God is able to raise dead things to life, it is first a story of Jesus—and, therefore, a story about a God—who is willing to join people in their pain, and...he...weeps.

According to John, this God weeps, and that is very good news for those who have experienced loss in their lives—so it's good news for everyone. Death, heartbreak, betrayal, and loss. These are some of life's greatest mysteries. There are 150 Psalms in the Bible, and over half of them are laments.[31] So it

---

31 Approximately 70 percent of the Psalms are laments. I find it interesting that approximately 0 percent of the top 150 worship songs sung in most churches are laments. I find that interesting and a big reason why many outside of Western

seems that humans have struggled with struggle for quite some time; what is interesting is that John 11 does not explain our pain; it simply reminds us that Jesus is so great that he works for us, and he is so good that *weeps* with us.

When I first became a pastor at nineteen years old, I felt like I always had to have answers for people. But the issue was I kept encountering suffering in other people's lives that I didn't have answers for. Like, what answer could I possibly give to the teen who was beaten by their father, what answer could I give to the mother who receives the call that her child was killed by a drunk driver, and what answer could I give to the son or daughter who prayed for their parent to survive cancer...and they didn't?

Have you ever experienced someone else's suffering that you don't have an answer for?

I've discovered that tragedy isn't what destroys people; tragedy *without meaning* destroys people.

So the longer I've been a pastor, the more I've realized that mystery is sort of baked into the human condition, and because of this, we often experience doubt. But I was always kind of taught that we need to get doubt out of the building. You know, like "faith and doubt can't coexist," they would say. Have you heard that before? But the issue is that, in John 11, Jesus wasn't moved because of their unwavering faith. You don't have funerals for those you still think are going to live again. Both Martha and Mary said, "If only you would have been there, Lazarus wouldn't have died." This doesn't scream unwavering faith, does it? Still, Jesus didn't seem offended by their doubt.

The longer I've been a pastor, the more I've realized that doubt seems to offend Christians far more than it offends Jesus.

Christianity don't see the Church as very helpful or relevant. The Church needs to reclaim lamenting as sacred.

But the Jesus story doesn't begin with a problem. It doesn't start with God sending a program or principles for a better life. The story begins with what theologians call *incarnation*. Which is a fancy-pants word that means, "God became human." So the story begins with how, in the middle of the great mystery humanity found itself in, the divine and human have come together.

It's a story about a God who enters into full humanity in order to lead us into our full humanity.

Jesus doesn't just enter into only certain parts of humanity. He meets us in the whole beautiful and messy thing. He meets us in love, joy, and wonder. But he also meets us in the struggle, the sobs, the heartbreak, and all those moments you shake your fists at the heavens in anger. And I think the reason that God enters into all parts of the human story is because God knew that even now there would be many people who are struggling to move forward.

I've heard people debate whether God exists.

But I don't think that is the most important question.

I think the most important question is, does God *care*?

Because if God exists but doesn't care, then who cares?

We don't care whether God exists as much as we wonder whether God cares. And I think that is why John includes the shortest verse in the Bible and tells us that Jesus wept at the tomb of Lazarus.

Because John wanted us to know that Jesus is with you in the mystery of pain and loss. Jesus meets us in our lowest places, and when he meets us there, Jesus does not scorn our grief; he actually steps into it with us, and he does this is because he knows that we will never find freedom from loss that we have not grieved.

After all, *pretending* to be free and actually *being free* are two different things.

Jesus does not want you to fake your freedom; he wants you to actually know and have a life of freedom, and grieving loss is one of those mysterious and powerful things that get you there.

Before Jesus resurrected on Sunday, he died on Friday. I think the progression of Jesus's resurrection is an example of how God works. God, in some mysterious way, can be found turning the tables on death and darkness and bringing new life from it. And I have met many Christians who only live their lives like every day is Sunday by refusing to make eye contact with brokenness, death, or sorrow. These are the people who claim to have never really known a life of pain. But it is equally unhealthy to live your life like every day is Friday. This is the person who has suffered, and that suffering is all they know. They are trapped in their pain because they are all wounds and no scars.

You'll never get to Sunday if you do not grieve Friday.

And when we grieve our Fridays, we discover that, just as Jesus was weeping at the tomb of Lazarus and just as the disciples would find out that God was actually purposefully moving through the death of Jesus on that Friday, we will discover that God is weeping with us and purposefully moving in and through our grief as well. But you'll never be able to write a better story if you remain stuck in chapter one.

Are you stuck on Friday?

Are there losses that you have yet to fully grieve?

The end of a chapter does not need to be the end of your story.

Have you been sitting down in a place called "angry" like Terah did?

Perhaps before you can fully follow where life is calling, you will need to learn from Terah and know that, if you are going to get your life unstuck, you may need to *recognize* and *release* those losses that have been ungrieved.

Chapter 7

199,416 Hours

"You are not a broken thing. You are a healing thing. Change the perspective."—Mike Foster

"When you lose the fight with vulnerability, you win your life back."—Brené Brown

199,416 hours.

That's about how long it took before I decided to stop sitting in a place called angry.

And it was one of the hardest and the best decisions I've ever made.

But before I talk to you about that, I want to talk to you about two other things that I believe will help you learn to stand again if you find yourself sitting, like Terah, in a place that's keeping you from responding to life's call. I want to talk to you about...

Kurt Cobain.
And shipwrecks.
Then I'll talk to you about how I learned to stand again.

First, let's talk about Kurt Cobain.

If you don't know who Nirvana is, I'm sorry. Someone who apparently doesn't love you very much has robbed you of some great music. You should stop right now and listen to Nirvana. Don't worry. I'll be here waiting.[32]

I'm serious. Do it.

Welcome back.

When I was in elementary school, one of my older sisters loved Nirvana, and sure enough, I got sucked in. There was just something so real about their music. Every time I listened to Nirvana, I felt the emotion that was being sung on every track. I was only a child when "Smells Like Teen Spirit" came out, but even at a young age, I remember being infatuated with the lead singer of Nirvana, Kurt Cobain.

I learned something interesting later: Nirvana felt so real to me because it was in fact coming from a very real place of pain for Kurt Cobain every time he sang. Kurt Cobain dealt with chronic pain much of his life. It was actually what he said ended up bringing him to use heroin—because it would numb the pain. Doctors never really figured out where the pain was coming from. But a lot of people have concluded that the same condition that caused him so much agony is the same thing that also caused him to sing the way that he did.

It was because he was in so much pain that he sang so uniquely—and you couldn't help but feel it when you listened.

And it was this that caused him to resonate with so many people. He sang from where it hurt the most, and because he sang from a very real place of pain, in a way, it helped others feel not so alone in theirs.

---

32 "Smells Like Teen Spirit" is a good place to start. But I would also recommend "Lithium" and "Heart-Shaped Box."

Kurt Cobain is an amazing picture of how pain can produce some of the most meaningful purposes in our lives. Often our best music, our best art, our greatest stories that others need to hear, come from the place where we felt the worst pain.

Are you with me?

Now, let's talk about shipwrecks.

There is a story in the Christian Scriptures about a man named Paul and a shipwreck he survived that he recorded in Acts 27 and 28. In this story, Paul finds himself somewhere he didn't ask to be and somewhere he didn't want to be.

Have you ever been there?

Have you ever been in a place of pain and thought to yourself, *I didn't ask for this, and I don't want to be here anymore*?

In Acts 27:20, Paul is on a boat and in the middle of a severe storm that had blotted out the sun and the stars. This was no drizzle or fog, which often blankets my home in San Francisco. This was the kind of storm that convinces you that all hope is lost. It's the kind of storm in which you can't see where you are going. It's the kind of storm that convinces you that you will be taken down to the bottom of the ocean and all hope is lost. And Paul didn't have some sort of clean-cut answer as to why he found himself in the storm he was in. Paul, who seemed to always have such insight from God, did not know why he was in the storm.

Now, pain is never fun, no matter what.

But isn't pain a lot easier to endure when you know there is a purpose for you on the other side?

For example, childbirth is anything but comfortable (or so I hear). But when you know that a beautiful child is on the other side of the pain, it makes enduring the pain easier (says the guy who has never actually pushed a baby out of his body. I have so much respect for all the mom's out there!).

I hate working out. It hurts and I'd rather eat tacos. But I know that, if I work out long enough, maybe one day Jena will look at me the same way she looks at Thor (curse you, Chris Hemsworth, and your godlike physique). So I endure another rep and walk funny for days because my legs are so sore from squats, and I do this because I can visualize a purpose for my pain.

But pain that seems pointless? Even worthless. That is the worst kind of pain, isn't it?

It seems to me that pain is not the greater destroyer of hope, but pain without purpose sure is.

And God didn't give Paul a reason for the pain he found himself in. But what God did was give Paul a *revelation*[33]; he assured him that he was with him and was leading him forward and that God would somehow bring purpose out of this storm. Spoiler alert: Paul and the crew did end up surviving the storm.

I know we all want reasons for our pain. I wish I could give you a reason for your depression. Or a reason for why they left you. A reason for the affair or a reason for why you got laid off or why your parent died of cancer. But what Paul learns, something we must learn as well, is that sometimes God won't give us a reason for our pain. Instead, God desires to give us something we need much more, and that is a revelation amid the pain.

A reason may explain your past, but only a revelation can create your future.

---

33 Acts 27:24

I know this might sound weird, but I'm not praying you'll receive a reason for your pain right now. I'm praying that you'll receive a revelation because a revelation will activate a hope within you that your pain can be used for great purpose. Paul didn't get *why* he was in pain, but God revealed to Paul *who* was leading him forward. Paul says, "Last night an angel of the God who I belong and who I serve stood beside me."[34] Paul says, I don't know why, but I do know *who*, and because of that, we're going to make it through.[35]

And he does make it through.

But not before the boat sinks and they are spit on the shore of an unknown island called Malta.

Because hope is possible, but hope is certainly not easy.

So Paul and the crew crawl onto dry ground, and just after they pull the last bit of seaweed out of their hair, they encounter the natives of Malta, and they built a fire for Paul and the crew. Things are finally looking up! But then Paul is laying sticks on the fire, and we're told in Acts 28:3 that, when he does this, a poisonous snake, driven out by the heat, bites Paul on the hand.

And Paul said, "Oh, hell nah!"

Okay, I don't know if he said that.

But he probably did. Trust me, I'm a pastor.

Paul was on a boat he didn't want to be on. In a storm he didn't want to be in. He was stranded on an island he didn't know. Then he was bitten by a snake he didn't see coming. And the snake didn't just nibble on Paul. One translation says that the snake "fastened itself on Paul's hand."

---

34 Acts 27:23
35 I used to be a rapper and because of this sometimes the rhymes just happen.

I think it's safe to say that Paul was having a terrible, horrible, no good, very bad day.

But then Paul did the most Chuck Norris thing that ever happens in the Bible. Verse 5 says that he 'shook off the snake.' How BA is that?

Can I pause and remind you of something about following life when it calls?

Life does not promise that the storms won't come.

It's doesn't promise that the ship won't ever sink or that snakes won't ever bite you.

But when you follow life when it calls, it will always give you the fortitude to endure the storm. Life will give you a shore to land on when the ship goes down. Life will offer the strength to shake off the snake when it strikes. Life does not mean the absence of pain. But when life calls, it gives you the power you'll need to keep going when pain is all you see.

Now, let me get to the end of Paul's adventure and why it matters for us. In Acts 28:7–8, Paul doesn't die from the snakebite, much to the surprise of the people of Malta. Paul was invited to the house of a man named Publius, who just so happened to be the chief official of Malta. Publius's father was deathly ill, and he thought, if Paul could survive a snakebite, maybe Paul possessed something that could help them in their darkest hour. So Paul went to this official's house, and we're told that Paul went in and prayed for him, and laying his hands on him, he healed him. Paul's *adversity* had turned into an *opportunity* that led to someone else's *healing*.

And how did Paul heal Publius's father? This is the best part.

He healed him by laying his *hands* on him.

The same hand that was bitten by the snake was the same hand God used to heal someone in need.

Please tell me you're letting that sink in.

Paul was shipwrecked, lost, and bitten. And all of this pain was positioning Paul to be the source for a miracle in the life of someone else. God turned the disaster into destiny. The wreck into a revival. The bite into a blessing.

Only God.

From Kurt Cobain's greatest pain, great music was born.

From Paul's greatest pain, greater purpose was achieved.

So the question that you must ask if you are going to learn from the haunting story of Terah and stand up from the place of pain you've been sitting in is not whether you will experience great pain in your lifetime. If you are going to love deeply and live fully, then you will experience deep pain. So the better question is, what will you do when you find yourself in the place of your greatest pain?

Because you and I have something in common. And that is that we cannot choose our pain, but we can choose our *response* to our pain. What you decide to do with your greatest pain is no one else's decision but yours, and what you decide to do with your pain will ultimately determine whether your pain will be useless or useful.

The reason for your pain does not determine your future; only your *response* to your pain does that.

Paul stood up in his pain, and God used it for greater purposes.

Terah sat down in his pain, and he stayed there until he died.

Two different responses to pain led to two entirely different outcomes.

So how will you respond to your pain?

This is why 199,416 hours will always be a significant number for me, personally.

199,416 hours.

8,309 days.

272 months.

22 years.

Those number matter to me because that's how long it took before I shared my story of how I was sexually abused as a child, and that is how long it would take before I decided to no longer sit in this place of pain for one more moment.

For twenty-two years, the only people who knew about my abuse were me and my abusers. I thought that it would stay that way until the day I died. I was supposed to trust my abusers, so I began to believe that lie that those you think you can trust will hurt you. So as a result of the agreement I made with this lie, I determined to do everything I could to be in control and to stay in control—because if I am in control, then I can't be hurt anymore. Being out of control is what my abusers took advantage of, so as a young boy, I decided to never let that happen again.

And it turns out, I got pretty good at being in control. From becoming Student Council President, to leading teams, to even leading my own church. If control was a drug, then I was a high-functioning addict.

My peers called it strong leadership.

My therapist calls it my primary mode of survival.

The irony is that my "leadership" was actually keeping me from moving forward. And my mode of "survival" was the very thing that was killing me. As I sat in my pain, I became a victim twice—a victim of what had been done to me and a victim of what I was doing to myself.

Terah was 205 years old when he died in a place called angry.

I was thirty-one, and for the last 199,416 hours, I had been sitting down in a place called abuse, and I too would die in this place if something didn't change. But one afternoon, I got something that I needed. No, it wasn't a reason. I still don't know why it happened, and I never will. But what I got was something I needed far more—a revelation. And that revelation was that God was with me and wanted to lead me forward to freedom. That God was able to turn the tables on my pain and transform it into purpose.

So I stood up.

I decided that this place called abuse was not going to be where I died.

I was home alone, and I wept every tear that for the past 199,416 hours; I had told myself I was not allowed to cry. I told my wife about my abuse, and she held me, told me it was going to be okay, and reminded me how much she loved me. I've since started seeing a therapist, and I am beginning the process of healing. It's like the door to the basement of my heart has been swung open, and in that basement was Travis, the little boy, who I'd kept locked up for twenty-two years in an effort to forget. And for the first time, that boy was seeing the light, and as his eyes squinted from the sudden burst of daylight he had not seen in years, he was finally walking out into freedom.

I haven't healed fully. I'm still working through a lot. But I can tell you this: I believe that my source of my greatest pain may just be music to someone's ears that helps them know they are not alone. My shipwreck may be some-one else's revival, and my snake-bitten hand can be a source of healing for others in pain.

Because I refuse to sit down in that place anymore. I refuse to settle there when life is calling me into the future. I refuse to allow the end of my story to end like Terah's.

I will not die in this place.

It took me 199,416 hours to stand up and start walking again.

What if right now you didn't sit for another minute longer either?

I believe in you. Even more, I believe God believes in you. And that God is with you, leading you forward, and that he isn't done with you.

So what if right now, wherever you are reading this, you decided that Terah's story will not be your story and decided to stand up and walk or, better yet, *run* into your future?

Chapter 8

Twenty Seconds of Courage

"Give me a stock clerk with a goal, and I will give you a man who will make history. Give me a man without a goal, and I will give you a stock clerk."—J.C. Penney

"Art is a human act, a generous contribution, something that might not work, and it is intended to change the recipient for the better, often causing a connection to happen. The most difficult part in choosing whether you want to make art is committing to what it requires of you."—Seth Godin

In the movie *We Bought a Zoo*, Matt Damon plays the role of a British writer, Benjamin Mee, who rescues a failing zoo while coming to terms with his life as a widower and single father. It was a really powerful story of someone overcoming life's obstacles and deciding to not give up on the future. One line in particular leapt off the screen and into my soul when I first heard it; it reminded me of what it will take if we are going to follow life when it calls.

Benjamin Mee said, "Sometimes all you need is twenty seconds of insane courage."

That's not just a great line from a well-written story. It is the sort of line that could change the story of your life if you believe it enough to do it. Sometimes all you need is twenty seconds of insane courage. For many, twenty seconds of courage would be a tipping point in their life that would take them from settling to embarking on the adventure that life is inviting them into. Twenty seconds of courage is enough to help you to cross that line called "conformity" and step into the unknown that life is calling you into.

I've only lived thirty-four years, and although there is much that I need to learn, I've discovered that, in your life, you will have many daily decisions, but you will only have a few *defining* decisions. Daily decisions are decisions like what will you wear, what show on Netflix will you watch, and whether you will take cream in your coffee (and for anyone who has any respect for coffee, the answer should be a clear and resounding no.).

Those are daily decisions, and none of those decisions will be decisions you remember on your death bed. But who you are going to marry, what career will you have, whether you will have kids—those are just a few major defining decisions that many of us will make. And while daily decisions may determine the course of your day, defining decisions will determine the course of your life, and you will spend the rest of your life managing those few defining decisions. So it is when you are faced with a defining decision that you will need those twenty seconds of insane courage to go where life is inviting you.

This brings us, one last time, back to the defining decision of Terah.

Sandwiched between two of the most epic biblical biographies—Noah and Abraham—is the story we've been reflecting on. It's a sad, and often un-known, story of a man who embarked on a journey, experienced great pain along the way, and eventually and sadly settled until the day that he died. It's a sobering story because all of us know a Terah or two, and if we're hon-est, all of us might be one defining decision away from becoming a Terah if we're not careful. All of us could find ourselves enslaved to a false identity or sitting down in the place of pain in our past, instead of running into a new place of possibility in our future.

Terah started his journey, but he didn't finish it because starting is the easiest part of any journey, while finishing is far more difficult. If finishing was easy, everyone would do it.

Don't believe me?

How many New Year's Resolutions have you fulfilled compared to the ones that went unfinished?

Exactly.
Me too.
Guilty as charged.

As a matter a fact, the last time I checked, only eight percent of people who start a New Year's resolution actually complete their resolution. I don't say that to shame you. My past is full of canceled gym memberships I said I would use, empty journals I said I'd write in, and stale nutrition bars I said I'd eat instead of Taco Bell. We need to talk about this because, until we accept our vulnerability to settle, we will likely describe our settling with more palatable and socially acceptable terms like the following:

It's time that I grow up.
I'm just being realistic.
I've decided to wait on God.
I think it's time to be more responsible.

When was the last time you heard someone say, "What am I doing? Oh, just making the defining decision to settle for the status quo for the rest of my life?"

Exactly.

No one says that and yet it happens every day.

Instead, we spin it with language that, on paper, might look like "wisdom," but in our hearts we know we are settling.

I'm not saying any of those things above are inherently bad. I am not advocating that you never grow up. But there is a difference between being childish and being childlike. I don't want you to be childish, but I never want you to give up on the hope, wonder, and whimsy of being childlike. After all, there was once a Middle Eastern rabbi saying that those with childlike faith would inherit what God is doing on earth.

What I am saying that, if we're not careful, we can use any of these socially acceptable ideas as makeup that we put on our fears to make them look a little more acceptable. What I am saying is that you won't ever break free from the status quo until you are willing to look your fears in the eyes and call them what they are. This is anything but safe, and this is anything but comfortable. But you'll never find the good things your soul craves by being safe; you'll only find them by being brave.

Those who engage life when it calls are not the best looking; they are not the wealthiest or the most popular. Those who engage life to the fullest are just the ones who decide to be brave instead of safe. They chose to move with courage instead of waiting for clarity. You see, destiny is far more a decision than it is a mystery, and no one settles on accident, and no one succeeds on accident.

No one.

Both success and failure happen as the defining decision to be safe or to be brave. I learned something a few years ago that I go back to all the time, especially in times of deep uncertainty. According to the Vedas, the ancient holy Scriptures of India, there are three operating principals at work in nature at all times. Those three operating principles are the following:

1. *Creation*, which is embodied by the deity Brahma.
2. *Preservation*, which is embodied by the deity Vishnu.
3. *Destruction*, which is embodied by the deity Shiva.

Brahma (creation) is seen as the force of progressive change, Vishnu (preservation) has one primary objective, and that is to nurture and protect that which is relevant, while Shiva (destruction) attacks and removes that which is irrelevant and unnecessary. Brahma—or Creation—is meant to be primary, in first position, the ultimate driving force in our lives. Vishnu—or Preservation—belongs in the second position, and Shiva—or Destruction—belongs in the third.

But here's the thing: When we take our foot off the creation accelerator and go from creating to coasting, when our lives become more about preservation and maintenance than creative risk, we knock Brahma/Creation off its perch and elevate Vishnu/Preservation into the primary position. As a result, we create conditions in our life that allow for Shiva, the Destroyer, to swoop in and shake things up.

Now, Shiva is often misunderstood.

Shiva is not a devil or a demon. When Shiva is in its proper place, Shiva represents a natural and healthy process similar to digestion in the body. Irrelevancies get cleared away without us having to give them much thought. So the thought is that, when things get bumpy and when things get shaken up in our lives, it's a sign that Shiva has been awakened. It's not that we drew a bad card or are an unlucky person or that the universe is against us. We've just gone on autopilot. We went to sleep.

And life wants us awake!

A disruption can often be life telling us something new is coming, that the old is being swept aside to make room for something new. Invitations into the new often show up in our lives as interruptions of the old. The universe is not punishing us; it's actually offering a loving, albeit sometimes stern, reminder to put Brahma back in the primary position, to step out of our comfort zone and to get back on the path of risk, creation, and newness.

The point is that we are engaging in a conversation that has been going on for generations all around the world with all types of people. The point is that, through all of these conversations, whether you are reading the story of Abraham or the holy Scriptures of India, we all seem to know on some level that, when we stop creating and start maintaining, our lives begin to experience a sort of disruption that serves as an existential alarm clock to our sleeping souls.

How weird and brilliant is it that the universe seems to be designed in such a way to push us towards being brave?

I don't know about you, but I think that's pretty great.

And that is why we need the story of Abraham—because Abraham gives us all permission to take the risk and to create. Abraham is an incredible example of someone who was brave enough to allow creativity to lead, instead of conformity. And it's his story that I want to lean into for the remainder of our time together, because it turns out that his story has withstood the test of time because his story is a glimpse into the messy and wonderful human story. Abraham rids all of us of our excuses for why we cannot follow life when it calls and empowers us with the courage to create instead of conforming.

Terah settled on the border of his destiny, but Abraham would learn from his father's mistake and finish what his father set out to do. But remember that Abraham didn't have more clarity, or even more capabilities, than Terah. The only ingredient Abraham possessed that Terah abandoned was courage when he was faced with the most defining decision of his life, and that was enough.

And courage is enough for you too if you are going to follow where life is calling you.

This of course means that you very well may be one defining decision away from your God-given destiny. You can decide to stay and ignore. Or you can decide to go and see where the life that is calling you will take you. One choice leads to a kind of destruction; the other leads to wonder and growth and hope. One choice may insulate you from the burden of fear, pain, and disappointment. But it will also insulate you from the power of breakthrough, love, and wonder.

Maybe you have a dream that keeps you up at night, but nobody gets it.

Maybe your life is full of well-intentioned people who think being safe is what is best for you.

Maybe you have a new way of doing something, but nobody has done it quite like that before.

Perhaps settling is tempting because it would be easier to conform to how it's always been done. Safe doesn't just seem simpler; sometimes doing the safe thing actually *is* simpler. That's why so many choose to follow the voice of safety rather than the voice of life.

Courage can be exhausting when so many people doubt you. Courage can be discouraging when so many people misunderstand your courage for crazy.

But the world is full of safe.

We are overstocked on enough status quo to last us a lifetime. The store-houses of "boring" are shelved to the ceiling. We don't need you to fit into the safe system. That system is full. We need people that are courageous enough to escape the system and show all of us it can be done.

Courage is in short supply.

We need more courage.

The future needs you to keep being courageous.

That's why I wrote this book. It's why Abraham's story matters—because he lived his life courageously (albeit not perfectly), and he shaped the world because of it.

Why can't you do the same?

Go ahead and write down all the reasons why that can't be you and then burn the list.

It might take years for the world to recognize that you weren't crazy. But don't let that stop you. Keep being courageous until the rest of the world catches up.

Because you were not wired for preservation or destruction to lead your life. You were created to create. You were wired for wonder. So let's courageously allow creation to take us by the hand and lead us the only direction that creation knows how to go—*forward*.

Your twenty seconds of courage start now.

Part Two:
The Path of the Curious

Chapter 9

The Process is the Point.

"The Bible is deep! I liked the parts where some character was once this, but he ended up becoming that. Like he'd be dissing Jesus, and then he ends up being a saint. That was cool."—Lil' Wayne

"And I am certain that God, who began the good work within you, will continue his work until it is finally finished."—Paul, Philippians 1:6, AD 62

I was 18 years old, months removed from graduating high school, and I had just completed a three-month-long music tour up and down the west coast. And I was about to do what every teenager says they can't wait to do.

I was moving out of my home.

I woke up that morning before the sun had risen, I packed up my remaining belongings, and I waited for my ride to the airport. I remember what I felt as I locked the door behind me and drove away from my home. I remember that I was pretty quiet on the way to the airport because my mind was being flooded with all the memories, good and bad, that "home" represented for me. There are only a couple moments in life that, when they happen, you know that your life is about to change forever. This was one of those moments for me.

I was moving away because I felt like life had called me and it was calling me to be a pastor and give my life to shaping people who will then go shape the world. I knew that, if I stayed home and stayed in the world I had grown very comfortable with, I would be tempted to settle for what was good instead of what was great. I would eventually drift toward standardization at the expense of imagination, and I couldn't live with that.

I remember once hearing a story about how the ancient Greek warriors would burn their boats upon arriving on enemy shores. They did this so that they would not have the option of turning back. To them, the only way out was forward. Most people have a Plan B, but these warriors decided to turn Plan B into kindling. Was this the wisest game plan? I'm not really sure, but you've got to give them credit because doing that takes guts.

What does that have to do with me moving away from home? Well, I guess you could say that this was my burning-the-boats moment.

I was leaving my home, my family, and even my state because life had called, and I wanted to make sure that turning back wasn't an option. I didn't have a fallback plan. There was no Plan B. Against the advice of some well-intentioned people in my life, I decided to go for broke.

I've learned something about life that is not only true for me or ancient Greek warriors but also true for you. Life belongs to those who are willing to brave the unknown. Life belongs to those who are willing to take any boat that will lead to compromise and turn it into ashes.

Life called, and I was determined to see where it led me. What I didn't know was that, when life called, it would lead me to a place called Carlinville, Illinois.[36]

---

36 Carlinville is a quaint little town in Illinois that likely has more roadkill than it has humans.

Have you ever heard of it? I doubt it. It is the sort of town that you think only exists on the set of Gilmore Girls.

The closest theater was thirty minutes away, and it only had two screens and popcorn that would make you feel like butter was oozing from your pores for days. The nearest mall was over an hour away. The population was about the same as my high school's. And on Wednesday's, my coworkers and I would go to McDonald's because it was apparently the thing "everyone did" on Wednesdays. They called it "McDonald's Wednesday."

We literally had a day dedicated to going to McDonald's.

Does it get any more #murica than that?

I found myself frustrated throughout this season of my life because I was sure that God had called me to make an impact and grow the next booming ministry. I thought this was going to be my big moment to prove what I could do as a big shot pastor. Ugh, I feel gross just typing that. The spiritualized ego I had was unreal. I thought God was calling me somewhere, and it felt like he'd led me to the middle of nowhere.

Ever been there?

Where you feel like you are heading somewhere and then it feels like life dropped you off in the middle of nowhere?

While I was here, finally someone was willing to give me, an eighteen year old still trying to grow a beard, a shot at ministry. I was brought on as the youth pastor to help start a youth group at a church in Gillespie, Illinois, for a whopping $25 a week. Jena and I were this newly married couple in a church where the average age was seventy years old. But we felt like life was calling us to do this, so we went for it.

Before we knew it, some students started showing up. The only problem was these students weren't the kind of students that this church wanted. These teens were what they would have labeled "troubled," and they came from even more troubling homes. They smelled, they had lice, they cussed, and they clearly had no respect for church "rules."

And. I. Loved. Them.

But after this ragtag group started to grow as we gathered in the church basement each week, the pastor became increasingly frustrated with me. Once he scolded me after a youth gathering because we weren't telling the students that they needed to tithe. I'm not entirely sure what the lint and two pennies in their pockets would have done for the church. But apparently, this was the top priority for the pastor. Turn these teens into tithers!

So as much as it ripped our hearts out, Jena and I knew that we couldn't stay in this position long. We had too strong of a conviction that *people* were Jesus's biggest priority—not their behavior and certainly not their tithe. After all, if God could create the universe with the sound of his voice, I think it is pretty safe to assume that this God was self-sufficient. So we decided to move on. I think often about each of those beautiful people we shared life with.

Although I was discouraged because I hadn't imagined my first opportunity as a pastor to be like that, life continued to call, and this time it led us to Arizona City, Arizona.[37] It was slightly bigger than Carlinville. And by slightly bigger, I mean they had a Starbucks and a Dollar Store, and most of the population had all of their teeth. Jena and I came on the staff of a church called Freedom Assembly. The pastor took a risk on a now twenty year old who was still struggling to grow a beard. I'll always be grateful because it would give me one of the greatest chapters of my life.

---

37 Unlike Carlinville, Arizona City had slightly more humans than roadkill. But not by much. They also had a market called "The OK Market." Not good. Not great. Just *OK*. It always lived up to its name.

We started a youth group called the Mosaic, and what began as twenty-five students quickly grew into a couple hundred. We met in a school, and we got kicked out because "there were too many students."

A school kicked us out because there were too many students.

The irony of that still makes me laugh.

But what was so cool about the Mosaic was that it was full of every kind of person you could imagine. We had churched kids, pot heads, gang members, teen moms, gothic kids, skaters, athletes, white kids, black kids, Hispanic kids, Indian kids, Asian kids—It was truly a mosaic.

In fact, I remember a youth pastor at another church in town tell me that he shut down his youth group because "one of those gothic kids showed up, and we weren't going to have *those kinds* of people in our youth ministry."

I told him with a smirk on my face, "Hey, I have great news! You don't need to shut down your youth group; all you need to do is send all those goth kids over to our youth group. We love gothic kids. We have the lights down really dark during worship. They'll love it!"

He didn't think that was funny.

But I was dead serious. Bring on the goths. We love them.

I learned during this season that not only was life calling me to shape people to go shape the world, but even more, I wanted to be around people who looked nothing like Jesus. I heard Pastor Andy Stanley once say, "Jesus liked people who were nothing like him, and people nothing like him really liked him." I like that. I discovered in this time that I wanted to give my life to helping people nothing like Jesus know that Jesus not only really liked them but loved them—even if they were goth kids.

But then we felt like life was calling me to leave Arizona City. Honestly, it made no sense. We were seeing something so special happening in the Mosaic. There were weeks when we had more students than our church had as a whole. More than that, we were seeing students who you never would have imagined stepping foot in a church start coming to be a part of the Mosaic. But I just couldn't shake that life was telling me it was time to move on.

So I did.

And it landed me at American Eagle selling denim jeans to soccer moms and trying to sell credit cards to college students.

This is where I would work for two years while I volunteered for free at a church. I felt like life had just "reverse-Draked" me. You know what that is, right? Drake said he started at the bottom and went to the top. Being reversed-Draked is when you go from the top to the bottom, and I felt like life had just kicked me down to the bottom.

I went from seeing lives changed to counting change.

I was frustrated and confused. Had I misunderstood something? Was God playing a cruel joke on me? I was certain that life had called me to leave the Mosaic, but this wasn't what I thought it would look like.

I was volunteering from 9:00 a.m. to around 5:00 p.m. at a different church, trying to make a life, and then from 5:30 p.m. to midnight, trying to make a living. After a year of this, the schedule had taken a toll on me, and even worse, it had taken a toll on my marriage.

I used to think being single and lonely would be the worst thing in life.

It turns out being married and lonely is far worse.

My wife and I were married, but we were living like roommates. I was a full-blown workaholic, I was empty, I had bottled up anger at God, and truthfully, I was in denial about my depression. So on the evening of our four-year anniversary, I exploded and had an emotional breakdown. I sat on our bed, and Jena gave me a present for our anniversary, and I gave her a nightmare in return when I told her I wanted a divorce. I said I wanted out of our marriage, and I wanted out of ministry because I could not take it anymore.

And then I walked out as she sobbed on the bed.

I had become a monster. A version of myself that I never thought I'd be. I mean, no one gets married and thinks they'll ever have a moment like that. But here I was. I hurt the person who loved me and who I loved also. Even as I walked out that door, I was thinking, *Travis, what the hell are you doing? Turn around! Go back!*

But I was full of shame, and shame can convince you that you're a failure. That I was nothing because I wasn't a pastor. That I had thrown away everything life had called me to years earlier.

Shame is a liar, and I fell for it, hook, line, and sinker.

Shame is like a sprinter. It moves fast. But luckily, my wife's love was a marathon runner because, when shame ran out of steam, Jena's love was there waiting for me. We've now been married almost fifteen years, and every day I thank God for her.

After a season of therapy and creating new boundaries, my perspective began to shift. While folding some jeans after American Eagle had closed, I felt like God whispered, "Travis, if I can't trust you to pastor people here at American Eagle, why should I trust you to pastor a church?"

I call this "The Holy Backhand" because that was what it was. God was smacking some sense into me.

That moment was a defining moment for me. The last place that I thought would ever be holy ground became holy ground. I think that's how God works a lot of the time. He meets us where we least expect it and turns that space into holy ground. I think God does it this way because, if he didn't, if he showed up when and where we expected, we would likely try to take the credit for ourselves. If God showed up according to our plans, we'd probably end up trusting our plans more than we actually trusted God. At least, I think that's how it would be with me.

But it was in this moment, in front of that shelf of denim jeans, that I realized that I had confused calling with titles. I realized it was not my context that was keeping me from where life was calling me; it was my ego. That little S.O.B. inside of me that likes to sabotage my life. I realized that something deep inside of me needed to change before anything around me would change.

So, from that point forward, I decided to become the pastor of American Eagle, and every coworker and customer was a part of the congregation. They didn't know it. But I did. And I was determined to serve, love, and mirror Jesus to them. And over time, I started having breakthroughs with each of my coworkers. One of my managers would schedule me to close with her because she said she felt like she could process with me and that I actually cared.

I did.

I was her undercover pastor, after all.

After this season, it felt like things started clicking back into place again. I was offered a job as the young adult's pastor at the church I got married in, and Jena and I started a ministry called "The Well," and this little group ended up growing into hundreds. It was beautiful. I was enjoying where life had me, but now for all the right reasons.

But even in the midst of this, both Jena and I knew we were wired to lead our own church one day. Little did we know that "one day" would come sooner than we thought, and little did we know that "one day" would lead us to one of the world's most influential cities.

San Francisco.

We visited San Francisco, and there was something about the city that just felt like home. It was a city where dreamers went to go make a life even if they scraped by just to make a living. It was a place that was innovating the future. It was a city that everyone told me was highly irreligious.

And it was irresistible.

We felt like life was calling us to start a church in San Francisco.

We were told that San Francisco was a "graveyard" for churches. But we couldn't help seeing the city as a garden, bursting with life and beauty, and we wanted to give our lives to being a part of the story of the city. So we packed up our lives, and Jena and I, along with twenty-three other people, burned our boats and moved to San Francisco. Life had called, and we were going to respond.

And eight years later, the church has grown into something beautiful. I get to work with a team of the greatest leaders I've ever known. Weekly, I get to hear stories of people being shaped by Jesus. My wife and I are more in love than ever, and we have a beautiful baby girl named Finley who is the coolest kid you'll ever meet.

Now I'm sitting here at my dinner table, with a can of Diet Mountain Dew in a quiet house, and I'm reflecting on all of this, and if I had the opportunity, here's what I would tell myself eighteen years ago on the way to the airport that day I left home:

I would tell that young kid that life is about the *journey*, not the destination.

It's about *becoming* more than *doing*.

And the real adventure God is inviting you into is one that goes inward, straight to the heart, because God wants to show you your truest self so that you can live your fullest life.

I would tell myself that life is not about perfection, but about progress.

This leads us back to Abraham, who is about to begin his journey. For thousands of years, the story of this elderly Middle Eastern man who responded to the whisper of life will serve as an icon of what it looks like to travel the winding and unpredictable path that life beckons all of us to walk—the path of *Lech-Lecha*.

So if you find yourself in a place in your life that feels pointless, let me encourage you that your path has a point. What you thought was a detour was actually divine. If you keep walking, you will discover that life was pulling you forward the entire time. You will find the process, oh that zig-zagging path, was not without purpose. But, like Abraham, life was always beckoning you forward. So let's follow the footprints of Abraham and let us see where life takes us.

Chapter 10

Scarecrows

"The Lord had said to Abraham, 'Go from your country, your people and your father's household to the land I will show you. I will make you into a great nation, and I will bless you; I will make your name great, and you will be a blessing. I will bless those who bless you, and whoever curses you I will curse; and all peoples on earth will be blessed through you.'"—Genesis 12:1-3

"I find your lack of faith— disturbing." —Darth Vader

So let's recap where we've come from.

Abraham's dad, Terah, set out on a journey to Canaan, and some believe that the call Abraham received from God was actually given to Terah first. But because Terah experienced pain and immense loss, at some point, instead of choosing the way of the pioneer, he chose the way of the settler and never reached his intended destination. Terah is a sobering reminder that, although we cannot mess up God's plans, we can very well miss our role in them. But now it seemed that whatever voice Terah had intended to follow to Canaan was now speaking to Abraham and inviting him to continue the journey.

And God spoke to Abraham and said this mysterious Hebrew word, *Lech-Lecha.*

Lech-Lecha is a Hebrew word that can mean, "Go to yourself."

So in Genesis 12, it is like God said, "Abraham, I know your father has settled, but you don't have to. Your family line does not need to determine your plot line. It is time to *Lech-Lecha*."

There are a few theories about what *Lech-Lecha* means, but the sheer mystery of the phrase itself (when so many other phrases could have been used) makes it clear that the journey that Abraham has begun is clearly more than a geographic one; it's an existential one. If this were simply a geographical journey, then other words could have and would have been used.

So why does God say *Lech-Lecha* (go to yourself)?

Many believe that, when God invited Abraham to "go," to *Lech-Lecha*, it was an invitation into an adventure of wonder and self-discovery. Lech-Lecha was Abraham's journey to discover his truest self. This is where the Jewish story begins, and I think one of the most beautiful parts of Jewish history is that it is a story that begins with an invitation inward.

Self-discovery is a gift that the Jewish tradition has given the world.[38]

Which means that, if you've ever left "home" to discover yourself, or if you've ever gone "soul searching," or if you've ever watched a movie about a character leaving what they've always known, breaking the rules of their tribe, and discovering themselves in the process (so...pretty much every movie), you have Abraham to thank for that. Perhaps one of the greatest gifts the Hebrews gave to the human story was the revolutionary idea that we could all live a fuller life by discovering our truest selves.

That's what Lech-Lecha was about and why Abraham's story matters. Not because Abraham was the first to hear the divine voice of life when it called but because Abraham was the first to *follow* the voice into the future. And

---

38 For more on the major contributions that Jewish people have made to the world, I highly recommend the book "The Gift of the Jews" by Thomas Cahill.

because Abraham said "yes" to life when it called, we have all been given permission to do the same.

Because before Abraham, this sort of thinking and this sort of decision to leave everything you had ever known was unheard of. You could even say it was scandalous to do this. Abraham matters because Abraham blazed a trail for all of us and showed us a new way to live, a new way to be human.

According to the story, God tells Abraham that he is going to need to leave three things behind if Abraham is going to reach "the land which I will show you"—we now know that the "land" was actually Abraham himself. God was showing Abraham the true Abraham, and if he was to follow where life was calling him, Abraham was going to have to leave behind where he had always been in order to reach where he was always meant to be.

God speaks to Abraham and says, "You will need to leave

Your *land*,
Your *birthplace*,
And your *father's house*."

And what we're about to discover is that these three places are all symbolic of deep ties that Abraham was going to have to cut in order for God to show Abraham who Abraham really was. These were Abraham's boats, and if he were to follow where life was calling him, then he would need to burn them all.

Now, this is relevant for us because we will discover that these three places represent the very real ties that keep all of us from discovering our whole and true selves if we do not cut them and leave them behind.

Abraham's story reminds us all that you don't get to experience the *new* unless you are willing to walk away from the *old*.

Abraham's story reminds us that faith is more like a staircase than an elevator.

I think sometimes we believe that faith somehow allows us to bypass all the steps of the journey and be transported to where we need to be. Just press the faith button, and away you go. But the journey of faith doesn't work that way. It didn't for Abraham, and it doesn't for you. Faith is you deciding to take the next step, leaving the previous ones behind even though you will never see the whole staircase. Those who wait for perfect clarity before taking a step of faith always stand still—waiting.

Clarity comes *after* action, not before it. If you have clarity on exactly what you should do before you act, it is likely because your moment has already passed you by. If clarity came before action, there would be no shortage of Abrahams on this earth. But it is only after you take steps of faith and look backward that you see with clarity the journey you were on and why.

Abraham teaches all of us that first you need to *step* and then you will begin to *see*.

Step and then see. This is the rhythm of faith.

When we get that out of order and try and see before we step, we end up setting up camp in Haran. For Abraham to follow where life was calling, he would need to learn from the mistake of his father and step forward into the unknown even though he did not know where this journey would take him.

When Jena and I decided to move to San Francisco to start a church, we did not have a lot in the way of clarity. We didn't know if we could launch a church in a city that was known as a "graveyard" for churches. We weren't sure how we'd raise enough money to do this. San Francisco, at that point, was the most expensive city to live in, just surpassing New York City. We were living comfortably in Arizona, paying $800 for a one-bedroom apartment. The same amount would rent a closet in San Francisco. We didn't know if any of our friends would actually decide to go with us. After all, why would they leave everything they had known to move to a new city, get new jobs, and start a new life in order to start a new church?

Oh, and did I mention that I was only *pretty sure* that this would all work out?

I know. It's a pretty compelling vision cast.

I love this story tucked in the Hebrew Scriptures in a book called 1 Samuel about a man named Jonathan, who also followed life when it called, went into battle against an entire army with only his armor-bearer by his side. The odds were not in his favor (does anyone get Hunger Games references anymore, or is it just my wife?). What I love about this moment in Jonathan's life is that, when he asked his armor-bearer to join him in what seemed like an impossible battle, he said, "Perhaps the Lord will help us."

Perhaps.

I'm sure that really comforted the armor bearer.

Jonathan was inviting the armor bearer to risk his life and fight this army that greatly outnumbered them, and all that Jonathan could offer was "perhaps." And the armor bearer actually went along with it. I don't know who was crazier: Jonathan for being willing to face the army or the armor bearer for being willing to follow Jonathan into battle on nothing but a "perhaps." But if you read the story—spoiler alert—Jonathan and the armor bearer were victorious that day. Buried underneath that "perhaps" was a promise from God that they would only unearth if they were willing to take the next step of faith and face the army.

I've heard it said before that, "when you ask God to move a mountain, he will give you a shovel." Faith is the willingness to dig into the perhaps of what is in front of you, and when you do, you'll find the *promise* beneath the *perhaps.*

I wonder how many promises we've left unearthed and unknown because they remain buried underneath the fear of our perhaps? How many promises have I missed because, when they showed up, they were disguised as perhaps?

Perhaps was all Jena and I had when we made the decision to make the move to San Francisco, but we wanted to see what could be possible if we stepped out in faith. So we did. We turned in our notices, circled a date on the calendar, and began to move forward in faith one step at a time. The reason I'll never forget this moment in my life is because of what would happen next.

At this point, I was both excited and terrified about taking this step of faith. Have you ever been in that place?

I was "exceriffied."[39]

If you've been there, you know exactly what I'm talking about.

And the thing that I was most fearful about was how we could afford to live in San Francisco. I felt the best use of my energy was to direct it all toward launching the church and not working another job to try and make ends meet. I didn't know whether this was selfish or not, but I decided to pray about it. I remember one night praying something along the lines of, "God, I know you can do all things. So here's what I'm asking. Please, somehow, provide a source of income that would allow me to be fully focused on this church. I really don't want to work retail anymore. Customers are too mean, and don't get me started on soccer moms. I'll do whatever you want, but if you could work it out for us to have what we need so that we can focus on what we need to do, that would be great. Amen." I ended that prayer feeling a little silly, if I'm honest. But I prayed it. It was done. And I went to bed.

Then I woke up the next morning to a text.

---

39 I promise that will be the last Dad joke.

A pastor had heard about our desire to start a church in San Francisco, and he wanted to learn more. Not thinking anything of it, I called him, and for the next hour or so, we talked, and I shared what I felt God had put on our hearts to do. This pastor then asked what I would need to get going, and without even a little hesitation, I said, "You can pay for our salary until the church can afford to pay us."

I immediately felt like a fool. Faith can sometimes look foolish, I suppose. But I closed my eyes and awaited his response.

He said, "Yeah, I think we can do that."

All of a sudden, the *perhaps* started looking more like a *promise.*

This church would go on to be our greatest ally and supporter. Without them, I'm not sure how we would have gotten to San Francisco, and I am not sure how we would have gotten the church started.

By the way, I'm not saying that this will be how it works for you. It hasn't always worked this way for me. Sometimes I pray and wonder if God even got the message.

But I am saying that, if I hadn't had the faith to move on "perhaps," I would have never seen that promise take place. When Jena and I decided to move on perhaps, it forced us to look at every opportunity and knock on every door. When I started believing that promises were underneath the perhaps, I went from playing defense to playing offense. Would I have gone to that conference to share about our church that happened to be the same conference this pastor and soon-to-be-partner would be attending? Would this pastor have generously invested in our church? Absolutely not.

If I hadn't moved on perhaps, I would have never gotten to the promise.

Moving on perhaps positioned me right where I needed to be to experience the promise.

I wonder if you are missing out on some promises because you have yet to move beyond the perhaps in front of you.

Think of it like a scarecrow.

If birds were smart, they would know that behind every scarecrow is the good stuff. But the image of the scarecrow is enough to scare them away from the goods that lie just on the other side of it.

Your perhaps is your scarecrow.

But what if, whenever you felt the fear of perhaps towering over you, you saw it as a sign that the good stuff God has for you was there waiting for you on the other side of your perhaps? What if, whenever you were faced with a perhaps, you became suspicious that something good was close at hand?

The good news I have for you is that you are much smarter than a bird. *Much* smarter. So move beyond the scarecrow. Cross the line of perhaps, and you'll find the promises of God waiting for you on the other side.

As we will soon see, this was what Abraham would have to do in order to step forward into the existential journey that life was calling him into. The journey of *Lech-Lecha*. To embark on this adventure that life was calling him into, he was going to need to move beyond his own "perhaps" and leave behind three things that would otherwise hold him back from reaching the truest version of himself that God was inviting him to know.

Before Abraham could see, he had to take a *step*.

Before Abraham could experience the promise, he had to move beyond his perhaps.

It would not be easy. It would take him away from three things what he'd always known and that no doubt made him feel safe. And the same is true for you reading this book. If the journey of faith were easy, then you would have done it by now.

You will need courage to step beyond your perhaps before you see the promise.

Notice in Genesis 12 that, when he made his promise to Abraham, God didn't lay out the entire plan. He simply said, "I *will* show you." Abraham would be shown the land, but first he would need to leave his land, birth-place, and father's house.

Abraham's story reminds me that, to follow life, you will often have to have courage before you have clarity. But with every courageous step forward, with every courageous step away from those places and people that keep you from your truest life and truest self, you will gain a little bit more clarity as God reveals the land he's always wanted to bring you to.

So let me remind you of something.

You are more courageous than you think.

Whether you are eighteen or seventy. If you have a pulse, you have a purpose.

So it's time to move beyond your perhaps and experience the promises waiting for you on the other side. You will need to leave the old behind if you want to experience the new. You will need to leave behind what you have always known in order to become who you were always meant to be.

Friend, life is on the other side of your perhaps, which means you're not waiting for life; life is waiting for *you*.

Chapter 11

Leaving the Land

*"God told Abraham: '**Leave your land**, your family, and your father's home for a land that I will show you'"* —*Genesis 12:1*

"The problem with putting it all on the line is that it might not work out. The problem with not putting it all on the line is that it will never (ever) change things for the better. Not much of a choice, I think. No risk, no art. No art, no reward."—*Seth Godin*

Life spoke to Abraham and invited him to leave his *land, family*, and *father's home*.

Which, if you think about it, seems backward, doesn't it?

Wouldn't the right sequence of events be that you leave your father's house, leave your family, *then* cross the borders of your land? But God said it was the other way around for Abraham. As we proceed, we'll discover that there is much more going on here. We'll discover the story beneath the story, as well as why Abraham's journey is relevant for you and me today.

So let's get started, shall we?

God tells Abraham to "leave your land." The Hebrew word for "land" is the word *eretz*, and this word shares a common root with the word for "will," *ratzon*.

This word *ratzon* means "will" and "desire."

So when God tells Abraham to "leave your land," God is really first inviting Abraham to leave behind what seems *natural*, what seems *safe*, and leave behind everything that makes him feel *comfortable*. Abraham was to leave behind his natural wills or desires. Genesis 12 was an invitation to Abraham, but it also could be seen as a *warning* to Abraham. A warning that, if he was going to say yes to the future that life was inviting him into, he would need to leave some things behind. If he was going to embark on this journey that life was inviting him into, a life that Abraham was created for, then Abraham would need to come out of the only life he had ever known.

Abraham was going to need to leave the *land*.

The land represented the things that made Abraham comfortable.
The land represented everything that made sense on paper.
The land represented that which was both linear and predictable.
The land represented a version of life that could be good, but it wouldn't be great.
The land represented all of the reasons Abraham should stay put.

When life called Abraham, it gave him only two options: to be brave or to be safe.

But the catch is that he couldn't be both.
And you can't be both brave and safe either.

Because, like Abraham, if you are going to follow life where it calls, you will need to leave behind the safety of the land you've known, and it will invite you to instead brave the waves that are uncomfortable, uncertain, and unpredictable—because it is only in this space that you will experience the unbelievable. There is no growth in the comfort zone, and there is no comfort in the growth zone. When life calls us forward, we will all have to ask this question: Would I rather grow and be uncomfortable or never grow but always be comfortable?

Leaving the land isn't easy.

And I can imagine that the only reason that God would tell Abraham that he would need to leave the land, all those things that make sense and are comfortable, is because God knew that our greatest adversary to our break-through is *inertia*.[40]

It reminds me of what George W. Cecil said: "On the Plains of Hesitation bleach the bones of countless millions who, at the Dawn of Victory, sat down to wait, and waiting—died!"

Those who follow life where it calls aren't the ones with good intentions. They are the ones who are willing to make a risky decision. They are the ones who set the deadline. They are the ones who chose to be brave over safe because they know that, if they chose to stay in their land, to surrender to their the safety of their default will or desires, their bones would bleach on the Plains of Hesitation.

When Jena and I moved to San Francisco, we had a group of twenty-three others who had left their "land"—both literally and metaphorically—to be a part of starting a church. Twenty-three people left their homes to rent a one-bedroom apartment that would cost more than a mortgage in Arizona. They left family and friends they had known to be unknown in a new city. They left a good life in Arizona because they believed something great was happening in San Francisco, and they wanted in on it.[41]

---

40 Country music is a close second. But that's a different book.

41 One of the most common questions we received when moving to San Francisco is, "why would you do that?" I've learned that if you want to be a person that steps out in faith, you will have to get pretty used to that question. Faith will often look ridiculous to those watching from the sidelines.

What you might not know is that I asked more than twenty-three people to move to San Francisco. In the end, I had over thirty people say "yes." But not all of them made the trek to San Francisco. Over the last eight years, I've realized that there was only one difference between those who moved and those who didn't.

The difference wasn't a matter of time, talent, or opportunity.

The only difference between those who made the trip and those who didn't was one thing:

A deadline.[42]

The only difference between those who left their land and those who didn't was a simple deadline. And although setting a deadline is simple, it is anything but easy. Deadlines aren't easy because deadlines force you to rearrange your lives, deadlines create urgency, and deadlines require focus and sacrifice. You can always know how serious somebody is about a goal they have based on their deadlines. And those who made the move had done only one thing different than those who did not; they set deadlines and planned their lives accordingly. They took out the big red permanent marker and circled a day on their calendar and then proceeded to put in their two-week notices, sold most of what they had, packed in boxes what was left, and then scheduled their farewell parties.

Those who didn't make the move had all the *intentions* to move. They even had a *desire* to move. The difference between the two groups of people wasn't intentions or desire—it was a deadline. I discovered through this process that a desire without a deadline is a *daydream*. Because if intentions or desires were enough for people to accomplish their dreams and pursue where life was calling them, then everyone would be doing it.

---

42 And all of my Type-A and task-oriented readers rejoiced.

Why?

Well, my guess is it's because you can have good intentions, and you can have desire without actually being brave.

Talking about what you want to do is the easiest part.

But you can't set a deadline without being brave.
You can't sell the home.
Or pack the boxes.
Or quit the job.
Or say your farewells.
Or push through the doubters.
Without being brave.

You can either be brave or you can be safe, but you can't be both.

And the paradox of safety is that choosing a life of safety is the most dangerous thing you can do with your life. Because being safe in your "land," in the comfort of those wills and desires that you've always known, will be the very thing that keeps you from the future that life is inviting you into.

Being safe may keep you from hurt, but it will also keep you from experiencing hope.

Being safe may keep you from disappointment, but it will also keep you from your destiny.

Safety sells, but it never delivers on the hype because, in the end, it turns out that being safe is ironically quite a dangerous way to live.[43]

---

43 I have yet to meet someone grateful that they settled on their dreams. Have you? While they believed the cost of pursuing the dream was too great, they always discover the cost of safety was far greater.

Life will invite you to leave the land that make you feel safe, and it is only the brave who will pack their bags and cross the border into their destiny. It is only the brave ones that will leave behind the "land" of their default wills and desires in order to become their truest selves.

Abraham didn't realize that this single step of bravery was going to become the story he would tell and that this story would even outlive his own life—to the point that we are still talking about it today. Abraham did not know that his life would become the story that multiple generations would tell and would use as a source of inspiration. This reminds me of a sobering reality for all of us:

Everything you do or don't do will eventually be the story you tell.

When I was in my twenties, I wanted to be well known. I wanted to be the skinny jeans pastor that everyone followed on social media, the pastor that spoke at stadiums full of thousands, and a New York Times bestseller. I wanted to be well known. But now that I've gotten older and a little bit smarter and have come to terms that I don't look good in skinny jeans, I've realized that living to be well known is a hollow version of life. And now in my thirties, I don't desire to be well known as much as I want to be *known well*. I want to be known well by my wife and daughter, I want to be known well by those I pastor, and I want to be known well by my neighbors and community. I can be well known and not be known well, and I'm almost certain that, on my deathbed, I won't care about being well known; I'll care about being known well for my love of God and people.

So the question is, what kind of story do you want to tell with your life?[44]

_____

44 During pre-marital counseling that I do with couples, we will spend a great deal of time talking about their family narrative. The single-story that shapes and informs most of who we become. From there, we discuss what kind of story they want to tell in their family. The question that I will ask them to ponder is, "what story do you want your kids to tell when they describe their family?" So if you are stuck on the question, "What kind of story do you want to tell with your life?" Maybe ask yourself, "What

Do you want to be well known or do you want to be known well?

Abraham reminds us that the point of life is not to arrive safely at death. He reminds us that following life looks like pushing all of your chips to the center of the table. The story of Abraham reminds us that, just as Abraham's single act of courage to leave behind his "land" was enough to tip his life into the extraordinary, I believe you very well may be one decision away from a totally different life. And the key ingredient isn't your readiness; it is your *availability*.

If being ready were a prerequisite for God to move in a person's life, then no one would experience a move of God. The history of God's people is not a record of God searching the earth for fully ready and courageous men and women who can handle the task; it is a story of God transforming the hearts of cowards and the underdogs and equipping them with the courage and strength they'll need to be ready to follow life where it leads.

I think of what the wise King Solomon wrote in his book Ecclesiastes in the eleventh chapter. He said, "Farmers who wait for perfect weather never plant. If they watch every cloud, they never harvest."

To put it simply, the economy will never be perfect enough for you to be brave. The busyness of life will not just go away one day, leaving you with the margin you need to make your move. There will never be a point where you are one hundred percent insecurity and fear free so you can pack your bags, leave your land, and be brave. The timing will likely never be perfect. If you were waiting for those things to happen, go ahead and cross that off the list of "Reasons you're not doing what you're supposed to do." I am hoping that list is getting shorter for you.

You may not be ready, and that's okay.

---

kind of story would I want my kids to tell about me?" Sometimes you are one right question away from clarity.

You may feel uncomfortable or insecure, and that's okay. It may just mean that you are nearing the border of the "land" you have always known.

The question is will you be brave enough to be available and willing to pack up and leave the land?

The only difference between common people and those who are uncommon people is that uncommon people are willing to trek uncomfortable paths.

I think about Rosa Parks, who kicked off the Civil Rights movement by refusing to get out of her seat and move to the "colored" areas at the back of a Montgomery bus. Standing up to oppression would be painful, but she embraced the pain of it. Her life would never be the same. She didn't know where that single act of courage would take her, but she knew that staying put in a world of systematic racism was no longer an option. She was courageous enough to leave the "land."

Many years later, a journalist asked her why she picked that day to refuse cooperation with the systemic oppression of a segregated bus system. She said simply, "I was tired." The journalist filled in the blanks by asking if she was exhausted after working so hard all day and simply didn't have the energy to move. She responded, "Not that kind of tired...I was not tired physically, or no more tired than I usually was at the end of the day. I was not old, although some people have an image of me as being old then. I was forty-two. No, the only tired I was, was tired of giving in." Rosa Parks shows us that you will never create change until you reach the point where the pain of staying the same is greater than the pain of change.

Or have you heard the story of Desmond Doss?

Desmond's religion forbade him from carrying a gun or threatening another human life, which was very inconvenient when he was drafted into the Second World War. Doss was a conscientious objector, placed as a noncombatant, and was the target of ridicule from the other soldiers. But Desmond refused to stay in the land that, perhaps to others, seemed right, safe, or even logical.

He was serving as a field medic in Okinawa when the Japanese attacked his unit on top of a cliff, cutting down nearly every man. Desmond quickly rigged up a stretcher that could be lowered by a series of ropes and pulleys to the ground below. Then, by himself and under fire, he retrieved each soldier in his unit one at a time and lowered them to safety. President Truman, while presenting Doss with the Medal of Honor, mentioned that the medic had pulled seventy-five men to safety. I don't think Desmond did what he did in hopes of being well known. I think it was his deep commitment to being known well that compelled him to be brave in the face of great uncertainty. I believe it was his courage to leave behind the natural wills and desires that put him in a position to live his fullest life as his truest self.

I think about the missionary A.W. Milne, who set sail to serve and love the people in the New Hebrides in the South Pacific, knowing full well that the headhunters who lived there had martyred every missionary before him. But Milne did not fear for his life because he had already followed the call of Jesus to die to himself. Milne had already left the land of the safety of his default wills and desires. For thirty-five years, he lived among that tribe, and he loved them and served them. When he died, tribe members buried him in the middle of their village and wrote this on his tombstone: "When he came, there was no light. When he left, there was no darkness." His life would outlive his life.

Uncommon people are willing to trek uncomfortable paths.

It wasn't that they are necessarily smarter, wealthier, or more influential, but they were *brave*, and they were willing to cross the border of the land of comfort and safety, and now their lives serve as stories of hope that generations continue to tell. Uncommon people are more committed to be known well than being well known, and because of this, they could only live from conviction, not convenience.

So the question for you is, what *land* is life inviting you to leave?

What are those "desires" or "wills" that you must outgrow if you will need to leave behind if you are going to fully embrace where life is calling you?

What are the desires or wills that perhaps other well-intentioned people have given to you or projected on you that you will need to excuse yourself from to embrace this wild journey life is inviting you into?

Is it time to circle a date, make the deadline, and have your date with destiny? Is it time to stop letting "someday" stop you from doing what you can and must do today?

Faith is not holding the fort; it's crossing the border of safety, leaving your land, and venturing into the unknown. Faith, for far too many, is seen as a sort of insulation that protects us from danger. But what if faith is actually an invitation to become dangerous in the best sort of way?

What if faith looks more like leaving the land?[45]

As the writer of Hebrews once said, "Now faith is being sure we will get what we hope for. It is being sure of what we cannot see." I don't think it is a coincidence that, in Hebrews 11, a list of men and women of faith, Abraham gets the longest shoutout. Abraham was the one who blazed this trail for the rest of us who feel stuck in the land. Abraham showed us what faith looks like in action.

And faith looks brave.

---

45 By the way, can you imagine how much crap Abraham must have gotten by choosing to move beyond his natural will and desires? How many people likely thought he was either crazy or arrogant to assume that he could break the rules. It is easy to skip that tension, but it is a critical part of understanding the weight of what Abraham was being invited to do.

Abraham reminds all of us that we have two options. We can choose to stay and ignore life when it calls us. Or we can choose to leave the land that we've grown so comfortable with in order to discover the new land that God wants to show us.

What could be on the other side of the border of your land?

Will you be brave or safe?

What wills or desires must you outgrow and leave behind if you are to live your fullest life as your truest self?

Life is calling you to follow and find out.

Chapter 12

The Origin of Punk Rock

*"God told Abraham: 'Leave your land, **your family**, and your father's home for a land that I will show you'"* —Genesis 12:1

"To me, punk rock is the freedom to create, freedom to be successful, freedom to not be successful, freedom to be who you are. It's freedom."—Patti Smith

There was a man named Solomon Asch who wanted to run a series of studies that would document the power of conformity. Perhaps he did this out of personal interest or maybe solely for the purpose of depressing everyone who would ever read the results. I'm not sure.

In Asch's experiment, subjects were told that they would be taking part in a vision test, along with a handful of others. The participants were then shown pictures and individually asked to answer very simple and very obvious questions. The catch was that everybody else in the room other than one of the subjects was in on the experiment, and they were told to give the obviously wrong answers.

What was the point?

Solomon wanted to see if the subject would go against the crowd, even when the crowd was clearly and ridiculously wrong. Under the mounting pressure of having to break from the group, would a person crumble or stay strong?

One of the questions the subjects were asked to answer was a puzzle like the one shown below:

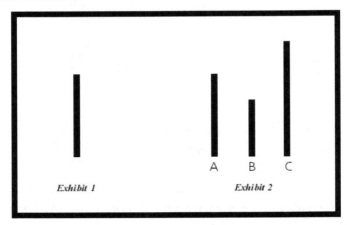

Exhibit 1   Exhibit 2

The task here was very simple. All they had to do was say which line on the right matched the line on the left. As you can see, Solomon wasn't asking people how to build a rocket ship. Honestly, the only way you could get the line question wrong was if, before answering the question, you put your fingers in a bowl of hot sauce and then proceeded to rub both of your eyes (which would have made this experiment way more awesome, but that's beside the point).[46]

Yet, thirty-two percent of subjects would answer incorrectly if they saw that the others in the classroom gave the same wrong answer. Even when the line was off by a few inches, it didn't matter. They would fall in line with whatever the rest of the group said.

In other words, one in three people would follow the group right off the proverbial cliff into the dark abyss of absurdity.

---

46 This happened once to me with some Taco Bell mild sauce that I discovered was on my finger only after I had rubbed my eye. Very. Painful.

So what does this have to do with Abraham and what it means to follow life when it calls? Well, when God calls Abraham, God not only invites him to travel the inward journey past his natural wills and desires—also known as the "land" he had been living in—but also invites Abraham to move beyond his "family." The Hebrew word for 'family' is *moledeth*.

And…wait for it…

This word translates to "family" in English, but it turns out that this word means so much more. Your "family"—your *moledeth*—is a reference to the *influence of home and society*. So to the first Hebrew audience, what they heard God say was, if you are going to *Lech-Lecha*, if you are going to journey to yourself and discover who you really are, then you are going to need to leave behind the two things that have shaped you and informed who you are the most.

What are these two things?

They are your place (your land) and your people (your family).

Are there two greater influences on the life of a person than the place you were raised and the people who raised you? Your place likely has with it certain stereotypes, political leanings, and so on. Why? Because every place has a story. You typically don't realize this until you experience a different story in a different place.

For example, I was born and raised in Arizona, but I didn't realize the story of my place until I left Arizona and moved to California—a different state with a very different story.
Arizona is historically conservative, and California is, well, definitely not that. I didn't realize how ethnically homogenous my place was until I moved to San Francisco, where I will hear five different languages while riding the bus.

In Arizona, a large percentage of citizens accept and affirm people of faith—in particular evangelicals. In Arizona, when I told people I was a pastor, they would respond with, "Wow! That's great. What an incredible way to spend your life!" But in San Francisco, because of terrible moments in history, like the assassination of Harvey Milk and cult leader Jim Jones, there is skepticism and cynicism about Christians—especially pastors. In San Francisco, if I mentioned that I was a pastor, I would be asked, "What kind of pastor? The kind we hate or the kind we can tolerate?"[47]

Every place has a story, and this matters because the story of my place has directly shaped the story of my life, and the same is true for you. If you want to understand why others are the way they are, take a look at their place.

But it's not only place that shapes us, because our people do as well.

I have yet to meet an emotionally unhealthy person who wasn't relationally unhealthy first. They go hand in hand. Has anyone ever carried pain that was not connected to a person in some way? Show me a happy person, and I'll show you a person with healthy relationships. Show me a hurting person, and I'll show you people who hurt them.

When I was a youth pastor and worked with teenagers, I recall a number of times that I would be told that so-and-so was such a "bad kid." But the closer I got to so-and-so, I realized that there is no such thing as bad kids; there are kids who were raised in bad places or by people who did bad things.

But no person is ever born bad—ever.

---

47 With that said, San Francisco is also often misunderstood as spiritually bankrupt. I could not disagree more. While my experience in Arizona is that while the majority are comfortable with religion, many (not all) are quite closed off to the mystery of spirituality. Just try and challenge religious tradition there and let me know how it goes. Yet, San Francisco, although many are not looking for religion, it is a city full of people who are more open to the wonder, mystery, and power of spirituality. So if you are a Christian who likes to compare San Francisco to Sodom and Gomorrah, it is not only bad theology but it just simply isn't true.

No one is born a murderer.
No one is born greedy.
No one is born a racist.
No one is born a materialist.
I have yet to ever meet a misogynistic baby.
Why? Because those behaviors are built, not bred.

Which means that no conviction has been developed in isolation. Not a single one. From your faith and your political leanings all the way down to the music you like listening to. You didn't just wake up one day with your convictions or ideals. Every single conviction you have—both good and bad—was shaped and informed by your place and by your people.

Have you ever noticed that it can be hard to change someone else's mind about a deep conviction? Have you ever wondered why that is so difficult, especially when someone holds a belief that is factually untrue?

I have two guesses as to why it is so difficult to change someone else's mind (including yours): *safety and belonging*.

At some point in your life, you were raised in a place and raised by people who told you, both implicitly and explicitly, that certain beliefs or ideals would keep you safe in a scary world.

Stay away from *those* people.
Vote for *that* political party.
Pray *this* prayer.
Practice *that* religious behavior.
Make *that* much money.
This is what it looks like to be successful.
Our family goes to *that* college.
And what's underneath all of this?

Safety.

If you do this, you will be safe. If you don't, you won't.

It makes sense why some people will fight for their convictions regardless of how wrong they might be. It makes sense that we have the ability to convince ourselves of almost anything, no matter how wrong it could be. Because it is not fact or fiction that is at stake—to them, it is their safety and belonging. And people will do anything and believe anything to protect their safety and sense of belonging to their place and their people.

Two areas of study tell us why: self-affirmation and cultural cognition. Both of these areas suggest that we cling to our views because our opinions have served as walls that keep the "good guys" (which conveniently are always those who hold your same convictions) inside and safe and keep the bad guys (who are, you know, all those dumb-dumb idiots who think differently than you) out and away.

So quite literally, our convictions are what we've been convinced will keep us safe and ensure that we belong.

I know this sounds pretty antithetical to the individualistic culture we've been raised in. I know that this might crush the idea that you are a unique little snowflake shaped by only God himself. And as much as you are a unique beautiful little snowflake, the reality is that your "personal convictions" aren't very *personal* at all. Those personal convictions have been handed down to you and then affirmed by many people.

This becomes even more clear when you have kids and you say something to your kid and think to yourself, "Oh my God. I sound just like my father." Why? Because you have convictions that are operating in your subconscious the entire time, which were put there by somebody else, and your subconscious works tirelessly to keep you in alignment with those deeply engrained values and beliefs in order to keep you safe.[48]

But our handed-down convictions aren't just about safety. They're also about belonging.

If you follow the code. Agree to the doctrine. Subscribe to our beliefs. Maintain our values. Then You are *in*. If not, if you break the code, don't agree with the doctrine, unsubscribe from a belief, or hold a different value—you're *out*. This is what we would call tribalism, and it's why people will hold tightly to a conviction—even if that conviction is proven to be empirically wrong.[49]

Have you ever wondered how someone could stay in a cult when you see it for the absurdity that it is?[50] Or why someone wouldn't just leave a gang that was clearly setting their life on a destructive trajectory? Or why an abused spouse would run back to their abuser?

Because the need to *belong* is that powerful.

James Clear, author of a great book called *Atomic Habits*, said it this way: "Humans are herd animals. We want to fit in, to bond with others, and to earn the respect and approval of our peers. Such inclinations are essential to our survival. For most of our evolutionary history, our ancestors lived in tribes. Becoming separated from the tribe—or worse, being cast out—was a death sentence."[51]

Additionally, Harvard psychologist Steven Pinker also said, "People are embraced or condemned according to their beliefs, so one function of the

---

48 I highly recommend the work by Dr. Caroline Leaf who speaks extensively on this topic.

49 Did I just describe American politics in two sentences?

50 Uh, hello QAnon.

51 Do yourself a big favor and go buy Atomic Habits.

mind may be to hold beliefs that bring the belief-holder the greatest number of allies, protectors, or disciples, rather than beliefs that are most likely to be true."

Simply put, we don't always believe things because they are correct.

Sometimes we believe things because they keep us *in* with the people we care the most about or who we believe will protect us.

False beliefs can be useful in a social sense even if they are not useful in a *factual* sense. We might call this approach "factually false but socially accurate." When we have to choose between the two, people often select friends and family over facts. This insight explains why we might hold our tongue at a dinner party or look the other way when our parents say something offensive or why we will rail against the political candidate with different beliefs while remaining silent on the shortcomings of the candidate who represents the values of our particular tribe.

Let me say it again. The human need to belong is *that* powerful.

This is why changing someone's mind can be an extremely lengthy and difficult process—because to the person you are trying to persuade, it can feel like you are doing more than asking them to change their mind; it can feel like you are also trying to convince them to change their *tribe*. If they abandon their beliefs and if they break the code, they believe that they are running the very real risk of losing their most important social ties. You can't expect someone to change their mind if you take away their community too. If you want to help someone change, then you have to also give them somewhere to go. You can't just give them facts; you have to provide them *family*—a tribe to belong to.

Absolutely nobody wants their worldview torn apart if loneliness is the outcome.[52]

With this in mind, it make sense that, when God asks Abraham to leave his family and to leave the influence of the place and now the people who raised him, God was very quick to promise Abraham that he would not be alone. God quickly assured Abraham that, on the other side of his leaving everything that had shaped and informed his life, a new tribe would be formed and that this tribe would change the world[53].

But in order to be a part of this new tribe, he would have to leave behind, not only the "land" of his natural wills and desires, but also all the convictions and beliefs that Abraham's people had handed down to him in order to be a part of this new tribe that would be a blessing to the entire world for generations to come.

In order for Abraham to follow life where it was leading him, he would have to break some rules, and he would need to be a pioneer for the right kind of anarchy. The kind that freed him from conformity to engage a life of creativity. Because in order for Abraham to embark on this journey, he would have to do the very thing that every human is terrified of doing—he would need to leave his place and his people.

Rolling Stone's Lester Bangs said, "Punk rock is lunging after some glimpse of a new and better world."

I like that.

---

52 If you don't believe me, just take a look at a high school kid who will follow people on a destructive path knowing that it isn't right and very well could cause harm to themselves. They will follow the crowd because many will risk having *unhealthy* relationships than risk not having any. Oh, and it's not just High School kids who do this.

53 Genesis 12:2–3

I like it because it sounds a lot like what God was inviting Abraham to do. Abraham was being invited to lunge after some glimpse of a new and better world, and he actually did it. I guess you could say that the story of Abraham might also be the origin of punk rock.[54]

Which means, of course, that, if you are going to follow life when it calls and where it calls you to go, you are going to need to be a little punk rock too. Life will invite you to lunge forward because there is a new and better world waiting for you. But you will need to break some rules to get there.

After this chapter, I hope you understand that the right question isn't whether a voice is informing you. You have been, and will continue to be, informed and shaped. So that's not a good question. The better question that you should be asking is, *what voice* will you allow to inform and shape you, and what sort of future is that voice inviting you into?

To follow life when it calls is to know that you will likely have to break some rules given to you by your place and people and you will have to challenge the status quo. Why was Abraham able to have so much influence without power?

Because Abraham dared to be different. He was willing to break away from his place and his people and everything that symbolized.

If you are going to follow life when it calls, you will have to confront the idols of the age. When God invited Abraham to leave his people and place, he was inviting Abraham to be free from the pressure to conform. Because those who follow life when it calls must be prepared not to follow the consensus.

One of the great writers on leadership, Warren Bennis, once wrote, "By the time we reach puberty, the world has shaped us to a greater extent than we realize. Our family, friends, and society in general have told us, by word

---

54 I have no doubt that Abraham loves The Ramones and Green Day.

and example, how to be. But people begin to become leaders the moment they decide for themselves how to be."

Let that sink in.

People begin to become leaders at that moment when they decide for themselves how to be. So who will be the voice that decides who you will become?

What rules do you need to break?

What lines do you need to cross over?

What values have you been told to follow in order to be "safe" that are actually putting you in danger of missing what life is inviting you into?

What place and what people do you need to leave behind in order to join the new world that God is inviting you into?

It's time to get a little punk rock.

It's time to lunge after that glimpse of a new and better world.

Rock on.

Chapter 13

Eighteen Inches to Freedom

*"God told Abraham: 'Leave your land, your family, **and your
father's home** for a land that I will show you'"*—*Genesis 12:1*

*"Our life depends on the kind of thoughts we nurture. If our
thoughts are peaceful, calm, meek, and kind, then that is what
our life is like. If our attention is turned to the circumstances in
which we live, we are drawn into a whirlpool of thoughts and
can have neither peace nor tranquility."*—*Unknown*

As Abraham begins his journey, God tells him that there will be three things
he will need to leave behind in order to reach the new land that God was
leading him to—which, just in case you have forgotten, is more than a
geographical reality; it's also an existential one. It is a journey for Abraham
into the fullest life by becoming his truest self.

And we're told that the last thing that Abraham needed to leave behind was
his "father's house." The Hebrew phrase *beit avicha,* "your father's house,"
refers to a person's *rational being* or their *mindset.*

So what God is saying to Abraham is, "Lastly, Abraham, if you are going
to discover what I'm trying to show you. If you are going to *Lech-Lecha* and
discover your true self and live the full life that you were created for, you
will need to leave that which makes you most comfortable, you will need
to leave behind the voices that call you to stay in that place of conformity,
and lastly, you will need to leave any broken mindsets or perspectives that

hinder you because, if you don't, it will keep you from reaching the land I'm taking you to." Abraham was going to need to leave his *place*, his *people*, and his *perspectives* so that God could give him a new place, new people, and new perspective.

Are you with me?

Leaving your "father's house" represented leaving all those unhelpful, unhealthy, and untrue perspectives and mindsets that keep us from where life is calling.

This brings us back to and finally explains the strange order of God's command we talked about earlier. Do you remember? When a person embarked on a journey, naturally the order would be as follows: he would leave his father's home, depart his family, and only then, leave the borders of his land. Yet when God commands Abraham, the order is reversed. Abraham is called to leave his land, then his family, and *then* his father's house. This is a subtle clue by the author to the reader that something else is going on here. Something deeper than Abraham's literal land, literal family, and literal father's house is being talked about.

And when we understand that something deeper is happening here, we can see that the path forward is the path we all must take if we are going to discover our truest selves and live our fullest lives. Often, people will wait for the world around them to change. But Abraham's journey reminds us that, before you can see any change in the world around you, there must be a change in the world *within* you. Before God does anything extraordinary around Abraham, God invites Abraham to allow God to do something extraordinary within Abraham.

Why?

Because as your *soul* changes, your *surroundings* do too.

We tend to believe it's the other way around, don't we? If we could just change our surroundings, *then* we could change our souls. Just ask someone how they are doing and listen to how quickly they will begin to rattle off all of the things happening *around them* as if those things are the truest metric of how well they are really doing.

So we ask, "how are you?" And they respond:

The job is excellent. I just got a promotion.
I finally started dating someone.
I'm no longer living check-to-check.
I've lost those last ten pounds.

And none of those things are bad things. But we all know it's possible to have it all together on the outside and still be falling apart on the inside. It appears that God knew this about us before we did, and Abraham's story reminds us that God prioritizes transforming your soul before changing your surroundings.

So that brings me back to you. I wonder if you've been living in your father's house for too long. I wonder if you've become a homebody in any broken or unhealthy perspectives that are keeping you from the fullest life and your truest self. I wonder if you have been waiting for God to change the world around you, and God is waiting on you to let him change the world within you.

I wonder, if you were honest, if there are any unhealthy or unhelpful mindsets or perspectives that are humming underneath the surface of your life that need to go if you are going to *Lech-Lecha* and go into yourself and follow life where it's calling you.

Abraham is referred to by the Jews as *Ha-Ivri* (literally "the Hebrew"), and the word *Ivri* is a reference to the word *avar* from *l'avor*—which means "to cross over." So Abraham is known as "the one who crossed over."

Abraham was the first to *cross over*.

He crossed over from existing to living.
He crossed over from conformity to creativity.
He crossed over from standardization to innovation.

So Abraham's story is about more than just him; it is actually a story about and for all of us. I wonder what it looks like when you are a person who crosses over as well. God seemed to believe that one of the lines Abraham would have to cross was leaving his old perspective behind and crossing the line into a totally new way of thinking.

And this is a journey we all must take if we are going to follow life when it calls us.

But here's the good news.

You are only about *eighteen inches* away from crossing over.

And the bad news?

Those eighteen inches will likely be the longest journey you'll ever take.

The journey I'm talking about is the journey from your mind to your heart. And the journey from your mind to your heart is perhaps the single longest journey you will take, but it's a road that must be traveled if you are going to follow life where it's calling you.

In Luke's gospel document, he quotes Jesus, saying that, just as a good tree bears good fruit and a bad tree bears bad fruit, so a heart will only produce what is within it.[55] The word Jesus uses here is the word *Kardia*, and this word is referring to far more than that organ that is busily pumping blood

---

55 Luke 6

throughout your body right now. *Kardia* means our true character, will, intention, and desires.

King Solomon once wrote in the Hebrew wisdom literature that, "as a man thinks in his heart, so is he".[56] Jesus apparently agrees.

So when God calls Abraham to leave his father's house and when Jesus talks to us about our hearts, they are both referencing the same powerful truth that is true for all of us: if your heart is the program, then your life will be the printout. Wherever your heart goes, your life will follow. As a man thinks in his heart, so is he.

When I refer to your mind, I'm not talking about the organ underneath your skull called the brain; I'm talking about the culmination of thoughts, desires, and mindsets that you bring with you into everything that you do. When those mindsets make the eighteen-inch journey to your heart, it is either producing a heart of health, identity, and love or your mindsets are producing a heart that keeps you from the full life you are created for.

So what God is telling Abraham and what Jesus echoes is that your life *starts* where your mind *sets*.

Before we ever do anything, we *think*. We are thinking beings before we are doing beings. When we wake up, our brains get to work building thoughts, and when we go to sleep, our brains begin to sort out those thoughts. Did you know that your brain actually generates more energy through electrical impulses in one day than all the cell phones on the planet? Your brain is literally working all of the time.

Just from reading that paragraph above, your brain generates electromagnetic, electrochemical, and quantum action in your neurons. It causes magnetic fields that can be measured, electrical impulses that can be tracked, chemical

---

56   Proverbs 23:7

effects that can be seen and measured, photons that can be activated and captured on computer screens, energy activity that can be explained using quantum physics, and vibrations in the membranes of the neurons that can be picked up by instrumentation.

All from reading just a few words.

So if anyone ever tells you to think before you speak or think before you act, remember that you can't *not* think before you speak or act. And if your words or actions are destructive, it's not because you're not thinking; it is because the *quality* of your thinking has led you to the outcome of your actions. You can't control whether you think, but you can control the *quality* of your thinking, and it turns out the quality of your thinking has a direct effect on the quality of your life.

Or as King Solomon said, as a man thinks in his heart, so is he.

God knew that your thoughts, desires, and mindsets would be so powerful that, if Abraham had any chance of reaching the land he was wanting to take him to, Abraham was going to need to leave behind the toxic and untrue mindset that he'd been living in for far too long. Because your life starts where your mind sets. So if you want to change your mindset, you will need to change where your mind sets.

Now, maybe all of the God language isn't your thing. I have good news. You can actually believe this whether you believe in God or not, because over the last few decades, the science community has learned that the brain is not static or fixed but is actually *neuroplastic*.

Neuro means "brain," and plastic means "change." So through neuroplasticity, a human brain has the ability to change throughout life. The human brain also has a unique ability to renew itself, and it does this through what is called neurogenesis. Neuro means *brain*, and genesis means *birth*. So essentially, through neurogenesis, every single day you have new baby nerve cells in your brain that are birthed and ready to receive whatever thoughts and information you give it.

For my Jesus people, this sheds a whole new light on the ancient writings of Jeremiah written around 586 BCE that says, "His mercies are new every day,"[57] as well as Paul's words when he says, "Be transformed by the renewing of your mind."[58] They were speaking to neurological realities that we would discover thousands of years later.

So whether you believe in God or not, this conversation matters. If the quality of our thoughts effects the quality of our life, then we need to do some serious thinking about our thinking. And if we are going to really think about our thinking, then we have to first realize that our thoughts are real things *in* us and they are doing real things *to* us. Every thought you have is an electrochemical event taking place in your nerve cells, producing a ripple effect of physiological changes. One article on this topic said the following:

"There are thousands upon thousands of receptors on each cell in our body. Each receptor is specific to one peptide, or protein. When we have feelings of anger, sadness, guilt, excitement, happiness or nervousness, each separate emotion releases its own flurry of neuropeptides. Those peptides surge through the body and connect with those receptors which change the structure of each cell as a whole. Where this gets interesting is when the cells actually divide. If a cell has been exposed to a certain peptide more than others, the new cell that is produced through its division will have more of the receptor that matches with that specific peptide. Likewise, the cell will also have fewer receptors for peptides that its mother/sister cell was not exposed to as often."

Confused? I get it.

---

57 Lamentation 3:23
58 Romans 12:2

In simpler terms, if you feed your mind with thoughts of negativity, you are literally programming your cells to receive the same negative peptides in the future. What's even worse is that you are lessening the number of receptors of positive peptides on the cells, which means you are making yourself more inclined toward negativity. This means the thoughts you are thinking right now are impacting all 75 to 100 trillion cells in your body.

This reminds me of the quote I once read from Peace Pilgrim that said, "If you realized how powerful your thoughts are, you would never think a negative thought."

So if the God of Abraham and what science has discovered are actually in agreement here, this means you have far more power over the quality of your life than you might have ever known. Maybe you have been thinking that you will never get better. The struggle will always be real. Perhaps you have even concluded that this is "just the way I am." I'm always going to be a pessimist. I'm always going to be negative. I'm always going to be sad. I'm always going to be fearful and anxious. But what the God of Abraham said and what modern science has confirmed is really, really, good news.

What is the good news?

That you are not done *growing*.

If what God invited Abraham to do and what modern science has proven to actually be possible in relation to the quality of our minds. Then this means that, every single day, you are the neuroplastician of your own mind, and the thoughts you think are your scalpel.

By the way, science and the Bible do not disagree that you have been born with certain predispositions. But what science and scripture are also agreeing on is that your predisposition does not have to be your destiny. You did not choose your predispositions, but every day, you have the ability to choose how you will think and react in response to those predispositions.

You may be thinking, "Well, Travis, you make it sound so simple." But let me remind you that just because it's simple does not mean it's easy. It wasn't simple for Abraham to leave his father's house of unhelpful or unhealthy mindsets, and it won't be easy for you to leave yours either. But just because it's not easy doesn't mean you cannot do it, and it certainly does not mean that you shouldn't do it. Most often, whatever is worth doing will rarely ever be easy.

If what scripture has said and science has confirmed is true, this means one of the most powerful and spiritual things you do every single day is *choose*.

You cannot choose what happens to you, but you can always choose how you react. And any time a negative train of thought arrives at the station of your mind, you have the freedom, the choice, and the power to not get on the train. Because you don't have to think about everything you feel, but I promise that you will *feel* everything you think about.

So, in a very literal way, every thought you have is taking up mental real estate. But here's the good news: you are not only a neuroplastician but also the landlord. And you have the power to evict any thought that needs to go. Why?

Because *you* are the landlord.

It's time to evict every toxic and unhelpful mindset and let a better, truer, more helpful mindset begin to take up residence.

Why must we do this? Because your life starts where your mind sets. As a man thinks, so is he. It's time to leave your father's house of toxic mindsets because life is calling you forward to a life of freedom.

Actor Joshua Radnor says it perfectly:

"A mind and heart untended to will just be a bundle of conditioned tics, hungers, fantasies, grievances, and neurotic thoughts on loop. We've not been properly trained to be suspicious of the voices in our heads. The world is a mess because of uninterrogated thoughts."

What mindsets do you need to interrogate?

What thought loops do you need to begin to break in order to be free and move forward?

What mindsets have overstayed their welcome and now need to be evicted?

Theologian and author C.S. Lewis once said that, if we want a field to produce a different crop, the change must go deeper than the surface. The field must be *plowed up* and *resown*.

What does it look like to begin to allow your thoughts and mindsets to be plowed up and resown?

Before Abraham could arrive at the new land God was about to show him, he had to leave his father's house behind. He had to leave those old, toxic, and unhelpful mindsets in the rearview mirror and decide to travel the arduous eighteen-inch journey from his head to his heart. Because this God wasn't interested in offering Abraham a slightly upgraded version of his old life.

He was offering him an entirely new life.

And God is offering you the same thing.

It's time to think about our thinking because our life starts where our mind sets.

Which means, for many of us, it is time to pack up and leave your father's house.

Part Three:
The Promise of Life

Chapter 14

Blindfolds and Blessings

"The Lord had said to Abram, "Leave your native country, your relatives, and your father's family, and **go to the land that I will show you**. *2 I will make you into a great nation. I will bless you and make you famous, and you will be a blessing to others. 3 I will bless those who bless you and curse those who treat you with contempt. All the families on earth will be blessed through you."—Genesis 12:1-3, NLT*

"Faith is taking the first step even when you don't see the whole staircase."—MLK Jr.

I want to tell you the story of when I kidnapped someone.

Calm down. It only happened one time.

I was young and in love and newly married to Jena, and for her birthday, I wanted to do something that she would never forget.

So I kidnapped her.[59]

Well, sort of.

---

59 Who said chivalry is dead?

She had never been to a live NBA game. So I bought tickets for seats that were so close to the court that you could identify the brand of deodorant the players were wearing. It was going to be great. Now, most husbands buy flowers, go to nice dinners, or write poems when they want to surprise their wife.

Not me.

I just kidnap them.

I'm a romantic. What can I say?

So when Jena came back home that day, I blindfolded her and told her that I was taking her somewhere and could not tell her where. She nervously agreed and got into my car, and I began to drive my blindfolded girlfriend to the arena. She asked for clues, but I remained completely silent for the entire drive in order to create a dramatic effect. And after about thirty minutes of silence, we arrived at the arena, parked, and I took the blindfold off of her. She was stunned to see us standing in front of the Phoenix Suns arena and me, her romantic abductor, standing there with two tickets in my hand.

I know what you're asking.

Why?

Why in the world am I telling you this story?

So, I was thinking about that story, and I realized something that is true when you're with someone you trust. You see, at no point did Jena get scared for her life. There was never a moment, while she was sitting there blindfolded and completely clueless about where she was being taken, that she began to worry for her future and pray that Liam Neeson would show up and save her. And even though my answers to her questions were vague and she did not know the plan that was unfolding, she never thought that

I had snapped and that her once-loving husband was now putting her in harm's way.

Why?

Because you don't need to know everything when you are with someone you trust.

Hold onto that thought because it's important. Now let's cut back to the story of Abraham.

As we have read, God calls Abraham to *Lech-Lecha*, to journey into himself, in order to discover who he really is. Abraham's story was about journeying toward identity and purpose. And in order to follow where life was calling him, Abraham would need to leave behind three things that had shaped and informed his life for the first seventy-five years of his existence on this orbiting ball we call Earth. He was going to need to leave behind his default instincts and that which made him feel most comfortable. God referred to this as Abraham's "country" or "land." He was going to need to leave behind the influence of his tribe. Also known as Abraham's "people." Then he was going to need to leave his deeply engrained mindsets in order to reach the destination that life was inviting him to journey toward. This was Abraham's "father's house."

But where was that destination, again?

If you're the planner type of person, it's likely that you already noticed this small detail and have been patiently waiting for me to address it.

God doesn't tell Abraham *where* he is taking him.

God calls Abraham to leave behind his place, people, and perspectives and simply assures Abraham that he'll show him along the way where the journey will take him. Sort of like being blindfolded. Abraham only knows that he is headed somewhere that he has never been and he is traveling beyond what he has always known in order to get there; he has no idea where "there" actually is.

But then God makes three promises to Abraham: I will make you a nation, I will give you influence, and I will give you purpose, so much so that your life will become *proof* to the world what God can do through those who trust him.

In other words, God assures Abraham that God's blessing will be greater than Abraham's sacrifice. If you leave your place, people, and perspectives, I will give you people and influence and purpose as you and your descendants will be a blessing to the world. So although God does not map out the destination for Abraham, in the end, God assures him that the reward he will be given will outweigh the risk that he has taken.

I believe this moment in Abraham's story matters because, in the ancient world of Abraham, doing what Abraham was being invited to do—leaving home, his people, and everything he knew behind—would likely result in risking his relationships, his influence, and would jeopardize the future of his family's story.

So if we brought this story into our world today, the typical objections to what God was calling Abraham to do would probably sound something like this:

But what if I am all alone?
But what will people think of me?
But what if I mess my entire future up?

If those three objections sound familiar to you, it's because they should. Aren't these three objections perhaps the three most common reasons that people use to avoid risk when life is inviting them into the unknown?

What if I take this risk and I lose people I care about?

What if I take this risk and people think I am crazy?
What if I take this risk, and I jeopardize my future?

It turns out that the core fears that humans often battle with haven't changed all that much, and before Abraham can even say a word, God speaks to these three objections, and God replaces every single objection with a promise to not only meet Abraham's needs but, even more, surpass Abraham's expectations. So God says the following:

You're afraid of being alone? I'll provide by creating *a nation through you.*

You're afraid of what people will think of you? I'll *give you more influence than you knew was possible.*

You're afraid of putting your future on the line? I will give your life so much purpose that it will be used as *proof* of what happens when people trust me.

But first, you will need to put on the blindfold, Abraham, and then we'll go. Because I'm taking you somewhere, but I'm not telling you where yet. You'll know when we get there. That's the deal.

On paper, Abraham had every reason to stay where he was and to decline the invitation of *Lech-Lecha,* and no one would have argued with him for staying put. People might have even commended Abraham for being logical by staying in his place, with his people, operating with the same old perspective. After all, the invitation of *Lech-Lecha* might work for an eighteen year old, but Abraham is seventy-five years old. Isn't that way too late in the game for someone to be taking these sort of risks? You've lived a good and long life, Abraham. Don't blow it now. Right?

But I believe that is kind of the point. Underneath each of these promises was a question that rang loud and clear not only to Abraham but to anyone willing to listen: "Will you take your one single life and take the risk and trust what I can do, or will you settle for what is safe and what has already been done?"

Because there are many people who don't move forward out of fear of being alone.

Because the majority of people won't put their reputation on the line.

Because, sadly, far too many choose existence over purpose.

Abraham knew this just as much, if not more, than anyone. Remember what happened to his dad, Terah? Abraham had a front row seat to what happens to someone when they decide to settle.

But the invitation of *Lech-Lecha* is an invitation to not be like the majority. It's an invitation to allow God to show you, you. This is what happens when you say "yes" and follow life on this journey of self-discovery: God assured Abraham that his sacrifices would pale in comparison to the promises he will receive as a result of his willingness to take the risk. If the reward is greater than the sacrifice, then was it really much of a sacrifice? This is the promise that God gives Abraham. Following where life was calling was going to require great risks, but it would lead to even greater rewards.

I believe the same is true for you too.

If you follow the invitation of *Lech-Lecha* and travel beyond safety, beyond the code of your tribe and beyond your current limiting mindsets, the rewards will far outweigh the risks. The benefits will eventually surpass the burdens.

For a season you may be alone, but in time, God will surround you with new people who will walk with you.

You will have critics that don't understand what you are doing. But God will tell a new story through you that is worth telling because you were willing to leave an old story that was worth leaving.

You may be leaving the safety of existence, but God will give you a purpose that will serve as proof of what happens when a person follows life when it calls them.

Right now, this chapter is happening in real time in my own life. I am hunkered down in a makeshift office that is actually just a small closet. Although I am somewhat introverted, I typically would not choose to work in a windowless closet that is so small, every time my daughter opens the door, it slams me on the back of my head. I'm pretty sure I've had three concussions by now. I am working in this closet right now because I, like the rest of the world this year, find myself in the middle of a global pandemic due to the Coronavirus. This pandemic has disrupted the lives of everyone across the globe and, for many, turned worlds upside down—including mine.

As I type this chapter, I am hours away from having to break the news to one of the staff members of our church that we are going to need to let them go, and in a couple days, I will have to have the same conversation with another person on our staff. Over the past couple weeks, I have wept in this closet with my hands over my mouth because I didn't want my daughter or wife to hear me. I have wept because, in a matter of months, this pandemic has seemed to undo the eight years of work that we have invested in building a church here. I am having to make excruciating decisions that affect people I love dearly. I have had more friends move away in these last couple of months than friends move in the past decade combined. I have never felt more alone, more defeated, and more helpless than I have felt in 2020.

And, like everyone else, I have no clue what the future holds. None. Zilch. Nada.

Maybe that's why I happen to be writing this very chapter at this very moment. Because Abraham's story is my story. Sure, Abraham wasn't walking through a global pandemic. But God was breaking Abraham down and disrupting his life at the deepest levels. Abraham knew that, after this encounter with God, his life would never be the same again. And, like Abraham, I feel as if I am being led into the future blindfolded. I know God is there, but he seems silent. Yet, I know that his silence does not mean his absence and that, if I continue to trust God's intentions for my life, I will eventually arrive safely, wherever God is taking me.

You see, the fact that God gives Abraham these promises *before* he has a moment to make any objection tells me something about God. It tells me that God has already worked out what I am worried about.

Maybe you need to just pause and say that out loud:

God has already worked out what I am worried about.

I am worried about the future of the church I pastor because of COVID. God has already worked out what I am worried about.

I am worried about not being able to provide for my family. God has already worked out what I am worried about.

I am worried that I will never have deep friendships that last. God has already worked out what I am worried about.

What are you worried about right now? What obstacles are in front of you, keeping you from stepping fully into the future that life is inviting you to experience? If Abraham's story is our story, then I can't tell you where God is taking you, but I can tell you that God has already worked out what you are worried about.

It reminds me of what Corrie Ten Boom once said: "If God sends us on strong paths, we are provided strong shoes." God will never call you to something and fail to equip you for the task. God is never improvising, and God is never intimidated. God knows the answer before you even ask a question. God never overpromises and under delivers. If God can create the cosmos with the sound of his voice, if God can somehow be present at the murder of Jesus, and if God can turn that murder into a miracle, then I think it's safe to say that God can be present even in a global pandemic and that God's hands are good hands to be in.

I have to believe that, if you have gotten this far into this book, it is because you have heard life call you to take the journey forward. Maybe life is inviting you to leave behind what your family has said you should be in order to realize who you really are. Or maybe you have found yourself in a faith community whose God is simply too small for you, and you know it's time to leave behind what you have always been told in order to encounter a more robust understanding and experience of God. Maybe for others it's leaving behind the security of a job you *can* do in order to pursue a calling that you were *made to* do. For some, it could be leaving behind a relationship that you're in because, before you can be the husband or wife you want to be, you need to first become the man or woman that you were created to be.

I am convinced that life is calling everyone, always.

But Abraham shows us that those who get to where life is calling them are not those who only wish for the rewards of faith; they are willing to take the risks of faith. Wishing takes no risk. Wishing is easy. Eventually you must go from wishing to working, and the path from wishing to working that we all must cross is a path called risk. No risk, no reward. Those who reach the right destination are willing to trust God enough to go from wishing to working by trekking across the path full of risks.

They are the ones who are willing to risk the crowd because they know God will provide a nation.

They are the ones who are willing to risk their reputation because they know God wants to tell a new story through their lives.

They are the ones who are willing to leave a life of safety because they know God wants to invite them into a life of significance.

They are the ones who are willing to be blindfolded and led somewhere they've never been before because they trust the God who is leading them. Why? Because they trust that, in some mysterious way, God has already worked out what they are worried about.

Back to the story that kicked off this chapter.

You know what's funny about the story of me blindfolding my wife and taking her to her first NBA game? I thought that this was going to be just a really fun experience, but it turned out to be far more than that. Now Jena is one of the biggest fans of basketball that I know. It's like, as soon as that blindfold came off, she experienced a whole new world that she would have never known had she only watched the game on TV. Why? Because there are simply some things that you have to experience for yourself, and when you do, nothing about your life is ever the same.

You are never the same.

Friend, life is calling you.

A new world is waiting to be experienced, and when you experience it, you will never be the same again.

The question is, do you trust God enough to put on the blindfold and follow?

"The Lord had said to Abraham, 'Go from your country, your people and your father's household to the land I will show you. **I will make you into a great nation, and I will bless you;** *I will make your name great, and you will be a blessing. I will bless those who bless you, and whoever curses you I will curse; and all peoples on earth will be blessed through you.'"*—Genesis 12:1-3

Anything with life in it can flourish only if it abandons itself to what lies beyond it. —Unknown

Jesus accomplished quite a few miracles during his ministry. Of course, the grand finale was the resurrection. It's hard to top that. But there is one miracle that Jesus accomplished that few seem to know about, and yet it is a miracle that, in my opinion, might be just as difficult as rising from the dead.

What miracle am I talking about?

One of Jesus's greatest miracles was having twelve best friends in his thirties.

I mean, that's pretty impressive.

You can't read through the writings of the gospel authors and conclude that Jesus wasn't relational. I think Jesus was the life of the party. I mean, remember his first miracle? He saved a party from ending too soon by turning water into wine. And it wasn't the cheap kind that I get from Target. Jesus gave them the *good* stuff.

I have no doubt that Jesus was the life of every party he attended. How do I know? Because throughout the Gospels, he kept getting invited to parties. You don't invite boring people to parties. I struggled early on in my faith because most Christians I knew didn't seem to think Jesus was any fun. It almost felt like the idea of a Jesus who laughs and cracks jokes is somehow less holy. But if God is the author of joy and if Jesus was God, then I have to believe that Jesus had to have been a fun and joyful person. Far too many images of Jesus are creepy. But Jesus wasn't creepy. How do I know? Because kids really liked Jesus, and kids don't like creeps.[60]

Jesus shows us that meaningful relationships are sacred.

But the life of Jesus also shows you that if you are going to follow life when it calls, there will be moments that life will lead you down lonely roads. Jesus had twelve best friends, but when it came time for Jesus to step into his calling and lay down his life, one of his friends betrayed him, ten of them abandoned him, and only one of the twelve was actually with Jesus in his final moments, although this isn't even for certain. Jesus shows us that when life calls you forward, don't be surprised if others choose to stay behind.

Perhaps this is why Jesus told us to count the cost if we were going to truly follow him into a full life?[61]

Jesus knew that great calling comes at a great cost.

---

60 Is it just me, or does anyone else get hyper-insecure when a child doesn't seem to like you? Like how lame am I if a four year doesn't like me?

61 Luke 14:28

If Jesus had listened to his twelve buddies, he wouldn't have fulfilled the purpose he had come to earth to accomplish. After all, his friends didn't want or think that Jesus should die. One time Jesus's friend Peter told him as much, and it didn't go over very well with Jesus. His friends wanted Jesus to be their militant and political leader that would finally stick it to Rome and restore Israel once-and-for-all. If Jesus chose to listen to the voice of his friends over the voice of life when it was calling, he would have missed his date with destiny. There came the point where he had to choose to follow his calling even though it meant doing so without his community.

The call of life will be costly. It was true for Jesus, and as we have already seen, it certainly was true for Abraham, who also left his people behind, and it will be true for you if you decide to follow life as well.

Have you ever stayed at a restaurant after it had closed?

If you are reading this and you are a server, you know who I am talking about because you hate those people.

But imagine with me that you and I went out to get some tacos together because tacos are the Lord's food. After we ate our meal and paid our bill, we just continued to sit at our table even though the server stopped refilling our soda two hours ago and three times has politely and passive-aggressively asked us, "Is there anything else I can help you with?" Now imagine that we stayed there so long that we got hungry again after the restaurant had closed, and we beckoned the server to our table and asked, "Hello, sir. Can we place another order?"

The server would reply, "I'm sorry, sir, the kitchen is closed."

If you are reading this and you were taught any manners, you are thinking that there would be no point in us sitting there that long. How rude. Go home, Travis. Why would you do that to that poor server? They are so going to spit in your taco, and you deserve it. Who would wait around and do something like that?

And you are absolutely right.

Which is my point.

Some people have been sitting in friendships that once were working and healthy but have now closed up shop. Perhaps you outgrew each other. Or maybe it was a toxic relationship that has only continued to wound you. Regardless of the situation, there are far too many people, while the other person has wiped up the tables and turned the "Closed" sign around, that they continue to remain there hoping for something amazing again. Yes, there are times when we need to stick out a hard time with a friend, forgive, and continue on. However, there are other times that life is trying to call us forward, but we remain stuck when we refuse to move on.

And before Abraham could become a nation, he had to leave some people behind. It was time to close up shop and move on. Life was calling him forward.

I've struggled with this chapter because I fear that you would misunderstand what I am saying. I worry that you will think that I am suggesting that you should use your friends and then lose them when they no longer serve you well. That is not what I am talking about. Please understand that if you treat people like commodities, you will never find community. At least, not a healthy community.

But there are times in all of our lives that life calls us forward, and this will mean at times leaving behind relationships that would otherwise keep us stuck in the status quo. They say that your closest friends are the greatest predictor of your future. If that is true, do you like where your future is headed? If not, life may be calling you forward, and it might be time to leave some people behind.

I recall the story that Mark recorded of Jesus raising a dead girl back to life. When he said that the girl was only sleeping, it said, "The crowd laughed at him. But he (Jesus) made them all leave." There were those in the room that could not handle what Jesus was doing, and before Jesus could get to work, he had to get the doubters out of the room.[62]

I wonder if there is anyone in your life right now that is not ready or equipped to handle where life is calling you?

Is it time to get them out of the room so you can get to work?

I know that's pretty heavy. Thank God that when God called Abraham to leave his people, He quickly promised Abraham that He would surround him with a nation. Although much was left behind, God assures Abraham that much more will be given to him in his future. Faith seems to complicate your life before it blesses your life. But when the blessing comes, it is always worth it.

When life calls you out of that church that serves a version of god that is far too small, it will hurt to leave them behind. But rest assured, God is bringing you new people that will walk with you.

When you decide to follow the voice of life calling you out of that abusive relationship you have felt trapped in, watch God raise up others to show up at just the right time.

When the voice of life invites you out of a broken cycle in your life, this might require you to leave those who would rather keep you stuck than see you succeed. But wait for it because God is bringing you new people who will champion your purpose instead of challenging it.

---

62 Mark 5:40

I feel like I can speak to this because when I first heard the voice of life calling me, it really complicated my life.

I was midway through high school, and for the first time, I came to trust that there was a God who not only existed but even more cared about me. I heard the voice of life, and it was calling me forward and into a life of purpose and hope. Little did I know that this moment would not only be a beautiful moment in my life but also a moment that would complicate my life. Because I knew after this encounter with this loving God that I would never, ever, be the same again, and something had to change. My two older sisters had already traveled deep into a dark spiral into drug addiction. Before this moment, I had begun my own downward trajectory with alcohol to numb my deep anger.

I remember going back to my friends and telling them that I was done drinking with them because I didn't like who I was becoming. I said to them that God had changed me, and I wasn't going back to how I used to live. One of my best friends was not happy about this decision, and he stood up and continued to shove and insult me for my newfound faith.

So I punched him in the mouth and told him that I was praying for him.

I was clearly still a work in progress.

But I knew after that night that life was calling me into a journey that my friends were not ready to go with me on. Little did I know that this would only be the beginning.

During this season of change, I moved out of my mom's house and began living with my dad, who recently came back into my life. Then I felt like it was best to move to a different high school. Partly because I had just gotten suspended (as I said, I was a work in progress), which only made it easier to decide to start fresh somewhere else, I knew life was calling me forward.

Still, I didn't realize how much I would leave behind before I could really move forward.

Life called

And then I lost all of my best friends.

I punched someone in the mouth.

I moved out of my mom's house.

Then I got suspended.

And lastly, I followed up by leaving my high school.

I remember sitting alone in the cafeteria on the first day at my new high school and wondering if I had just ruined everything. Did I misunderstand what God was telling me? I was trying to put myself in the best possible position to follow God wherever He was taking me, but now I'm stuck here eating my sandwich alone in a cafeteria, pretending to be waiting for friends that didn't currently exist.

I wonder if Abraham ever had moments after he had left everything, where he sat alone and asked what he had gotten himself into? I bet he did.

But what Abraham learned and what I would learn is that when life calls, it will complicate your life before it blesses it. Which I suppose is why it is faith that gets us through, and if you endure and keep following life where it is calling you, it has a funny way of replacing all that was lost in greater ways than you could ever imagine.

I don't know who or what might need to be left behind for you to move forward. But what I do know is that God is the ultimate promise-maker and promise-keeper. The question is, will we be promise-takers and promise-seekers?

The promise will come with a price. Sometimes that price is leaving behind the people and relationships that have closed up shop and moving on. It might mean uprooting yourself from all you know and walking a lonely path for a season. But what God promises Abraham, and I believe if this story is intended to be for all of us, then what God promises us as well is that this God will always follow through on His promises. And not only is God good for his promises, but his promises are always good. They will be exceedingly more than you could ever hope for or imagine.

Life may call you to leave behind your people.

But God will provide you a nation.

Not a bad deal if you ask me.

Chapter 16

The Problem with Mimes

*"The Lord had said to Abraham, 'Go from your country, your people and your father's household to the land I will show you. I will make you into a great nation, **and I will bless you; I will make your name great, and you will be a blessing.** I will bless those who bless you, and whoever curses you I will curse; and all peoples on earth will be blessed through you.'"— Genesis 12:1-3*

"The greater danger for most of us lies not in setting our aim too high and falling short, but in setting our aim too low and achieving our mark." —Michelangelo, Italian Renaissance painter, sculptor, architect, poet, and engineer

What would you be willing to risk your reputation for?

I have found that there are far too many people who don't have an answer to that question, or they have never seriously thought about it. There are countless blogs, books, and voices that advise us on ways to *build* our reputation, but few on risking it.

Yet, it appears that a great risk precedes every great chapter in history. This seems to also be true for each human individually. Show me a person who lived with great purpose, and I'll show you a person who paid a great price.

Consider the story of street vendor Mohamed Bouazizi, who was trying to survive the oppression that Tunisians were being crushed under at the hand of a corrupt dictator. But Mohamed Bouazizi would become one of the inspirational people who changed the world when he set himself on fire out of desperation in December 2010. He became a symbol of the suffering of all Tunisians. Bouazizi's death would represent the oppressed, and his life would spark nationwide unrest that resulted in the overthrow of Tunisian dictator Zine El Abidine Ben Ali. The Tunisian uprising, in turn, led to the Arab Spring movement that ultimately toppled regimes in Egypt and Libya.

The world will never be the same due to Nelson Mandela, an anti-apartheid activist, and leader of the African National Congress who, in his early political career, was imprisoned for 27 years for political agitation against the South African government. Yet his willingness to take extreme risks galvanized the cause for racial equality, and he endured to become the nation's first black president, a Nobel Peace Prize recipient, and an international symbol of freedom.

Of course, living a life of purpose will not always cost you your life or your freedom. But that doesn't make them any less meaningful. Take, for example, the story of a single mother living on welfare. She worked on an outline of her book for over five years and was rejected by nearly every publisher. No one thought her book would sell, and they thought young boys would never buy a book written by a woman. But J.K. Rowling risked not only her reputation but her livelihood and refused to quit, and after Bloomsbury Publishing in London decided to pick up *Harry Potter and the Philosopher's Stone*, the Harry Potter series would become a worldwide phenomenon that changed the publishing industry.

What each of these stories reminds me of is that ordinary people have the capacity to live out extraordinary purposes when they are willing to embrace risk. If there is a bridge between dreaming and doing, that bridge is called *risk*, and it is the bridge we must all cross if we are to go from simply dreaming to doing what life is inviting you to do.

This, again, is what makes the story of Abraham so extraordinary. Abraham was being invited to leave everyone he knows and everything he knew to follow where life was leading him. It was a call that came with great risk, and this is likely why God quickly assures Abraham that if he is willing to take this risk, God will tell a story through Abraham that will be a blessing to the world.

If Abraham was going to do what no one else was doing, he would need to think in ways that no one was thinking. And this would risk not only his livelihood but also his reputation. For Abraham to experience all that life had in store for him, he would have to choose between seeking God's face or worrying about saving face. God promises that he would make Abraham's name great. But Abraham would first need to be willing to lay down his reputation. When Abraham did this, he would learn that this single decision to take the risk would tip his life from the ordinary into the extraordinary.

I wonder if you may be one risky decision away from crossing over from who you are to who you were always created to be?

I wonder if you were to give your risk a name, what would it be? What is the risk that is keeping you from saying "yes" to the voice of life?

One of my favorite stories in the Gospels is in Matthew's document involving one of Jesus's disciples, Peter. If you know anything about Peter, you know that he was like your drunk uncle that you never quite knew what he would do or say when he came over for dinner.

Peter was unpredictable, emotional, and seemed to do very little thinking before he did something. So it is not surprising that Peter would be the only one to volunteer to jump out of his boat in the middle of a storm to attempt to walk on water towards Jesus, who had appeared to the disciples walking on water himself. Matthew records the story and says this:

Meanwhile, the disciples were in trouble far away from land, for a strong wind had risen, and they were fighting heavy waves. About three o'clock in the morning, Jesus came toward them, walking on water. When the disciples saw him walking on water, they were terrified. In their fear, they cried out, "It's a ghost!"

But Jesus spoke to them at once. "Don't be afraid," he said. "Take courage. I am here!"

Then Peter called to him, "Lord, if it's really you, tell me to come to you, walking on water."

"Yes, come," Jesus said.

So Peter went over the side of the boat and walked on water toward Jesus. But when he saw the strong wind and the waves, he was terrified and began to sink. "Save me, Lord!" he shouted.

Jesus immediately reached out and grabbed him. "You have so little faith," Jesus said. "Why did you doubt me?"[63]

What struck me as I read this isn't that Peter began to sink in the water, but rather what *caused* Peter to sink. Matthew writes that after Peter took a couple of steps on top of the water, what caused Peter to sink was that "he saw the strong *wind*.»

I think that is strange.

Because the last time I checked, you can't *see* the wind.

You can hear the wind.
You can feel the wind.
But you can't *see* the wind.

---

63 *Matthew 24:24-31*

And Matthew tells us that it was what Peter *couldn't see* that caused his faith to begin to sink.

Peter's story reminds me of the one time that a mime trapped my wife in an invisible box.

The legend goes that Jena was just a little girl, and one day while she was at a fair, she encountered her first mime. Little did she know that this moment would scar her for the rest of her life. The mime chose Jena out of the crowd to be a volunteer, and then the mime placed her in an invisible box. The mime then walked around the "box," placing his hands on the invisible walls of the invisible box, and Jena began to panic. She was convinced that this would be the last time she would ever be with her family. She was now forever going to be trapped within this mime's box, and she would survive only on the invisible food that would be served on an invisible tray that the mime would slide under the invisible door.

I believe it was when Jena began to cry that the mime set her free. Jena is a very loving person, but she now hates mimes and she has never forgiven the mime community of their crimes against her. Pray for Jena.

While Jena could leave that invisible box whenever she wanted, something convinced her that she was stuck forever. Just like Peter, what she *couldn't see* became a barrier that kept her from freedom.

And that's why this story in Matthew thumps. Because we are all like Peter and Jena at times, aren't we? Who hasn't felt led to take a step of faith, and just as you were about to go for it, you began to fear all of the things that you cannot see. Who hasn't felt completely trapped at some point in your life but, looking back later, you realize that you weren't as trapped as it may have felt in the moment?

I have found that it is not something that *has happened* that stops most people from stepping into their future in faith, but something that *might happen*.

It is the winds of insecurity that rage against our hearts and the howling of the winds of fear that cause us to tremble that seem to cause many of us to take our eyes off of where we were meant to go and causes us to sink into the deep waters of mediocrity.

I can only imagine how strong the wind was blowing when Abraham heard life call him to leave everything behind and follow God into an unknown future. What made Abraham so extraordinary was not that he didn't ever experience fear or risk but that he moved beyond the fear of risk. It is not that Abraham did not have fears, but Abraham did not allow his fears to *have him* that took him from ordinary to extraordinary.

Have you ever heard of Joshua Chamberlain?

Joshua Chamberlain was a student of theology and a professor of rhetoric. If you asked him, the last thing he would have known himself as was a soldier. But when it came time to fight for his country, Chamberlain answered the call. He eventually became the colonel of the 20th Maine Volunteer Infantry Regiment, Union Army.

On July 2, 1863, Chamberlain and his three hundred soldier regiment were all that stood between the Confederates and inevitable defeat at a battlefield in Gettysburg, Pennsylvania. At 2:30 p.m., the 15th and 47th Alabama infantry regiments of the Confederate army charged, but Chamberlain and his men courageously held their ground. Then followed a second, third, fourth, and fifth charge. By the last order, only eighty blues were still standing. It appeared that the battle might be lost. Even Chamberlain himself had been struck down by a bullet that hit his belt buckle, but the thirty-four-year-old schoolteacher got right back up.

This was his moment. Would he retreat, or would he advance? Would he choose safety, or would he risk his life for the sake of victory?

When Sergeant Tozier broke the news to Chamberlain that no reinforcements were coming and his men were down to one round of ammunition per soldier, Chamberlain knew he needed to act decisively. Their lookout informed Colonel Chamberlain that the Confederates were forming rank in preparation for another attack. At that point, the rational thing to do with hardly any ammunition and no reinforcements would have been to surrender. The stakes were high, and the unknowns were even higher. No one would have blamed him if he had chosen to surrender.

But Chamberlain wasn't wired that way.

Joshua Chamberlain made a decision that would turn the tide of the war and single-handedly save the Union. Chamberlain climbed onto their barricade of stones in full view of the enemy and gave a single command. He pointed his sword and yelled, "Charge!" His men then started running at the Confederate army, which vastly outnumbered them.

They caught them off guard, and in what ranks as one of the most unlikely victories in military history, eighty Union soldiers captured *four thousand* Confederates in only five minutes. What seemed like a suicide mission saved the Union.

Historians believe that if Chamberlain had not charged, the rebels would have gained the high ground. If the rebels had gained the high ground, there is a good chance they would have won the Battle of Gettysburg. If the rebels had won that battle, the historical consensus is that the Confederates would have won the war. One man's courage not only saved the day, but it also saved the war and, as a result, saved the Union.

In his later years, Chamberlain would reflect on the war with these words: *"I had deep within me the inability to do nothing. I knew I may die, but I also knew that I would not die with a bullet in my back."*

Talk about risk.

Like Joshua Chamberlain, Abraham did not know what awaited him on the other side of his courageous decision to follow where life was calling him. But Abraham made a choice, that if he was going to fail, that he would fail gloriously. He would rather fail at pursuing something great than succeed at pursuing something safe.

And what Abraham would come to find out is not only would he be rewarded for taking the risk but that the reward would be far greater than the risk itself.

But he would never know until he was willing to go.

Abraham wouldn't know what God was doing until he was willing to go and see for himself.

Peter would have never known if he could walk on water until he was willing to go and step outside of his boat.

And you will never know what life has for you until you go as well.

The path that leads to a full life is littered with risks. But here's something I have come to learn about risk. I don't believe risk transports you to where you need to be as much as it *transforms* you into who you are meant to be. Remember, Abraham's story is much more about transformation than destinations because God is far more concerned about who you are becoming than where you are going.

So by not taking the risk.

Or by staying in the boat.

Or by remaining trapped in the box.

Or by staying where you've always been.

The greatest loss will not be that you do not reach where you were meant to go. The greatest loss is that you will never become who you were always meant to be.

And the world needs you to become who you were always created to be.

It was only after Abraham was willing to risk the story he had always known that God would write an entirely new story through his life. And God assures Abraham that when this new and true story about Abraham is written, he will not only be famous, but his story would be a blessing to the world.

And here we are, thousands of years later, still talking about his story.

Let me say it again.

The world needs you to become who you were always meant to be.

The world needs people who are living out the stories that God has always desired to write through their lives. Because when the world gets the *you* that you were always meant to be, all of us will be better because of it, and the risks will have been worth it.

Chapter 17

How to Live like Taylor Swift

"The Lord had said to Abraham, 'Go from your country, your people and your father's household to the land I will show you. I will make you into a great nation, and I will bless you; I will make your name great, and you will be a blessing. **I will bless those who bless you, and whoever curses you I will curse;** *and all peoples on earth will be blessed through you.'"—Genesis 12:1-3*

"It is not the critic who counts; not the man who points out how the strong man stumbles, or where the doer of deeds could have done them better. The credit belongs to the man who is actually in the arena, whose face is marred by dust and sweat and blood; who strives valiantly; who errs, who comes short again and again, because there is no effort without error and shortcoming; but who does actually strive to do the deeds; who knows great enthusiasms, the great devotions; who spends himself in a worthy cause; who at the best knows in the end the triumph of high achievement, and who at the worst, if he fails, at least fails while daring greatly, so that his place shall never be with those cold and timid souls who neither know victory nor defeat."—Teddy Roosevelt

So it turns out that there are a lot of thoughts about this particular promise that God will bless those who bless Abraham and curse those who treated Abraham with contempt. For Jews all around the world, this verse holds a significant and sacred meaning because this verse speaks to them of a God who was wholly committed to them as a people. So before I go further, I don't want to diminish that or get lost in the weeds of what others may think this verse is or is not saying. I want to stick to a very simple truth that is being communicated to Abraham: if you are going to follow life when it calls, if you are going to accept the invitation of *Lech-Lecha* and journey into yourself, some people are going to love you for what you're doing, and some are going to hate you for it. Along the journey that life has you on, some will bless you, and others will curse you. Follow life long enough, and you will have fans, and you will also have your fair share of haters.

Or in the words of the great prophet Taylor Swift, "Haters gonna hate, hate, hate, hate, hate…"[64]

Your ability to shake off the haters is going to be crucial if you are going to follow where life is calling you.

I once heard author, Seth Godin, say that it is okay to accept applause, but you get yourself into trouble when you *expect* applause. Why? Because haters always seem to come out of the woodwork when you start doing something that matters. Perhaps haters don't want you to pursue your dreams because it only reveals that they aren't pursuing theirs. Misery not only loves company but, more than that, seems to try and recruit it. And before Abraham is to take the journey that life is inviting him into, he is warned that he will have fans, and he will have haters, and he's told to not obsess about either of them.

Instead, Abraham must remain focused on what is most pressing instead of who he is impressing. Why? Because focusing our attention on who we are impressing is the quickest way to lose our way.

Have you ever been in a car accident?

---

64 Don't act like you don't like that song. Curse you and your catchy hooks, Taylor.

I have, and I remember every single detail like it happened yesterday.

I'll be honest, I'm not sure if I ever told my dad the truth about this accident. I believe I told him that someone backed into me in a parking lot. If you are reading this, Dad, I'm sorry.

But I was seventeen years old, and I was currently in a serious "friend-lationship" with my eventual wife, Jena. What is a friend-lationship? It's that stage in a relationship where you tell everyone, and attempt to convince yourself, that you are "just friends" with the person you are totally and obviously interested in. When you are in a friend-lationship, it is painfully and annoyingly obvious to the rest of the world that you two are totally into each other, no matter how much you deny it.

Friend-lationship.

That's where Jena and I were, and I want to apologize to all my friends for all the times I lied and told them that she was just a friend, even though I talked to her every night and laughed at every joke she made, and flirted with her nonstop.

Back to the story.

Jena and I were driving together, and although I can't remember exactly what we were debating about, I know that I was right about whatever it was. I remember I had said some flirtatious comment to Jena, and she said something along the lines of "Oh, I'm sure that you say that to impress all the girls." Now I was getting onto my freeway exit, and I remember that I looked at her after this comment and channeled my deepest and most sexy Marvin Gaye voice I could conjure up. I said to her "Girl...you are the only one that I am trying to impress."

But before she could respond to the serious game I was dropping, I didn't realize the car in front of me had stopped, and before I could slam on my breaks I crashed into the car in front of me.

Seriously…how did I get Jena to decide to marry me?

My first car accident came the moment I took my eyes off of where I was going—because I was desperately attempting to impress Jena.

I have found that I'm not the only one who has experienced such a crash.

There are many others who have crashed in pursuit of where life was calling them, and they crashed because they took their eyes off the road and got distracted trying to impress someone else. I've counseled countless people who felt life was calling them to take a risk, but because they kept their eyes on impressing their parents, they crashed. I've witnessed story after story of people who were on the road toward where life was calling them suddenly crashing because someone told them that they didn't have what it takes, and they decided to take their eyes off of the road. They were on their way and on the road to their dream, but one critic, one bad review, one angry email, or one bad experience caused them to take their eyes off the road, and they crashed, and they still feel the effects of the whiplash years later.

It seems to me that one of the quickest ways to wreck your dream is to obsess about the haters.

Now, let me make an important side note: not everyone who disagrees with you or doesn't get your dream is a hater.

To write off anyone and everyone who doesn't get or who doesn't agree with your dream is immature. You can hear what someone has to say, but when you try and listen to everyone, then you are headed for a crash. I can *hear* everyone, but I don't have to and shouldn't *listen* to everyone. Especially when I listen to someone who isn't going anywhere themselves. I've had my fair share of people tell me "don't" throughout the years. Not all of them were haters, but many of them were. And I decided early on in my life that I would never let people who *won't* tell me *don't*. If they won't pursue where life is calling them, why should I listen to them when they tell me not to pursue mine?

If they won't pursue big dreams, I won't listen when they tell me, "Don't."
If they won't take risks, I won't listen when they tell me, "Don't."
If they won't listen to life when it calls them, I won't listen when they tell me, "Don't."

I will never let people who *won't* tell me *don't* and neither should you.

Misery may love company, but I don't have to show up to that party, and neither do you.

Like Teddy Roosevelt said, "It is not the critic who counts...But the man who is actually in the arena." Or I think of what Paul Simon said: "Blessed are the sat upon, spat upon, ratted on." Why are the sat upon, spat upon, and ratted upon blessed? Because if you have haters, then congratulations—it just means you're doing something that matters. In this life, you can either be judged or ignored. There is no doubt that being judged is uncomfortable. But if you are going to follow life where it leads you, get ready to be misunderstood, underestimated, and unfairly rejected.

Your alternative is, of course, much safer: do nothing and be ignored. But by now, we should all know that just because it's safer doesn't mean it's better.

One thing that rarely gets talked about outside of Jewish circles is how Abraham was the original iconoclast.[65] Abraham lived in a polytheistic world and was the first to embrace monotheism—the belief that there was only one God. As a pastor, I have learned, if I want to get some haters, all

---

65 An Iconoclast is "a person who attacks cherished beliefs or institutions."

I need to do is challenge a religious institution or tradition. So I empathize with Abraham on this one.

I remember when I got my first tattoo; in the church that I was employed at, that was a big no-no. At this time, many believed that pastors don't get tattoos, and it was usually backed up by some misused verse in Leviticus. So when I stood on stage with my new tattoo, you would have thought I had "I love Satan" tattooed on my forehead. I remember, one lady told me that I was "only good for street ministry now." All from a tattoo on my forearm.

Now imagine being Abraham, who didn't get some ink but was challenging the way the entire world understood, thought about, and talked about God.

You better believe he had some haters.

As a matter a fact, according to Jewish teachings, Abraham was raised by a father who was not only a polytheist but an idol merchant. So the belief was that Abraham's dad not only worshipped many gods but also made his living off of selling the existence of multiple gods to others. So when Abraham challenges polytheism, he is not only threatening a deeply engrained and embraced view of God but also threatening the very livelihood of his family.

Rabbi Nachman said this: "Abraham did not become distracted by all those who deviated from God's path...not even his own father. Now anyone who wishes to initiate a life of spiritual service [must do similarly]...paying no heed to a person who is an obstacle...[even if it is one's] father or a mother, in-laws, spouse or children...The same is the case with the obstacles one faces from the rest of the world, from those who ridicule and mock, tempting and preventing one from fulfilling God's true service."

So according to Rabbi Nachman, Abraham's greatest feat, the cause of his success, was his ability to embrace being the one who blazes a new trail that no one else is willing to or wants to walk down. Abraham was willing to be alone and singular in his focus; Abraham is cast here as a great rebel who is forever breaking free from the idols of his society—Abraham was the original iconoclast. More relevant for us, Rabbi Nachman says that Abraham is the model for anyone who wishes to follow life where and when it calls us.

Now, if you know anything about Rabbi Nachman, it is not surprising that these words come from him. He is remembered as a highly creative and highly unconventional leader who often found himself at odds with other Jewish leaders, including his own family members. But this teaching is also very modern and existential in its interpretation: strive to discover who you truly are as God invited Abraham to do. This is best attained by hearing many but not listening to everybody, including those considered to be experts or authorities. Because to follow life where it calls requires you to challenge some systems and crush some idols and ignore some haters. You will need to follow Abraham in his iconoclastic footsteps and commit to being singular in your focus even when the haters get loud.

After all, has any revolution come by maintaining the status quo?

Why would it be any different for the existential revolution that God is inviting each of us to experience? The future belongs to the iconoclasts who dare to challenge what has always been, to courageously pursue what could be.

I figured this chapter might be one of the more discouraging ones.

Who wants haters, after all?

I'm certainly not advising that you assume everyone is a hater or will eventually be a hater. I'm not suggesting that you should live your life as a proverbial bull in a china shop that bulldozes through anyone who might see things differently than you. But what Abraham's story reminds us of is that, if you are going to follow life where it is calling, you will have haters who try to get in the way. But, just like it was for Abraham, if you will continue to follow life into the future, God will protect you along the way.

God tells Abraham that he will bless those who bless him and curse those who curse him. I interpret that to mean that we don't need to obsess about our fans or our haters because God is in control.

Don't let the applause go to your head and don't let the hate get to your heart.

Trust God with both and stay focused on the journey that life has you on.

Keep your eyes on the road.

I love the story of Heisman Trophy winner Marcus Mariota from Oregon. To win the Heisman Trophy means a panel of more than 800 college football experts from around the country voted he was the best player in the 2014–2015 season. It's really an incredible accomplishment, but what few know—and what is most surprising about it—is how many schools offered Mariota a scholarship to play football. There are over 120 Division 1 football programs. So you would imagine that, since he was named the best player in all of college football that year, he must have been bursting at the seams with scholarships, right? So out of the over 120 schools that could have offered him a scholarship, how many actually did?

One.

The only school to offer Mariota a scholarship was Oregon. Part of the reason is, he lived in Hawaii, and despite the number of players that island has produced, it still remains largely overlooked in recruiting circles. But Mariota had one dream, and that was to play football at the highest level, and up until the 2014–2015 season, he had been largely overlooked by the majority of schools. He refused to be deterred by those who didn't see what he saw in his future; he kept going and refused to listen to what others were saying about him.

Now you may never play football.
You may never be a quarterback.

You likely won't be winning the Heisman Trophy.

But like Mariota, if you are going to pursue your dream, then you need to know that there will be many people who will overlook you. There will be people who ignore you, doubt you, and perhaps even hate on the dreams you are pursuing. You might pursue your dream and have 119 that curse you and one that blesses you. That's what happened to Marcus, and this moment in Abraham's life reminds us that, if you are going to follow life when it calls you, it will likely happen to you to at some point.

When the haters show up and the doubters start talking, here's what I want you to remember:

You don't need the haters to appreciate your dream in order for you to pursue it.
You don't need the haters to understand your dream in order for you to pursue it.
You don't need the haters to be impressed by your dream in order for you to pursue it.

What you need to do is keep throwing the passes when no one is watching. You need to write the book no one sees. Write the songs that no one hears. Keep building the business that no one appreciates yet. Because overnight successes are only the result of years of hard work and focus as you keep your eyes locked on the important work life is calling you to do, instead of who you are impressing along the way.

If Abraham's story and God's promise to protect him tell us anything about following life when it calls, they should remind us all that you don't need to impress everyone in order to leave a legacy behind that impacts everyone.

Keep your eyes on the road.

Chapter 18

The Power of Cupcakes

"The Lord had said to Abraham, 'Go from your country, your people and your father's household to the land I will show you. I will make you into a great nation, and I will bless you; I will make your name great, and you will be a blessing. I will bless those who bless you, and whoever curses you I will curse; and all peoples on earth will be blessed through you.'"—*Genesis 12:1-3*

"I am a little pencil in the hand of a writing God who is sending a love letter to the world."—*St. Teresa of Calcutta*

I am a total Apple fanboy.[66]

While the technology they have created is brilliant, what I find so interesting about Apple is their ability to speak directly to culture through their products. There is no greater example of this than how the late Steve Jobs and the people of Apple Inc. brilliantly understood the spirit of our age—a spirit of unfettered individualism and freedom—by marketing many of their products by using the prefix *i*.

---

66 I must, for the sake of my integrity, confess that for a brief window of time I ditched my iPhone for a Pixel. But my God is greater than my sin and I now have an iPhone again. Thank you to everyone who graciously walked with me during this very dark moment in my life.

iPhones.

iMacs.

iPads.

And I am pretty sure, if Apple made an iToilet, I would buy one. Sign me up.

Apple didn't invent narcissism, but they sure recognized it and leveraged it, and we'll stand in line and go into debt to be a part of it.

But while we may live in an iWorld and the iWorld might create great phones, computers, and tablets, there is one thing the iWorld can never create, as hard as it may try.

The iWorld can never create a greater future worth fighting for.

Because narcissism or selfishness cannot create a better future—only selfless and sacrificial love can do that.

The opposite of love is not hate, as many might assume. The opposite of love is *selfishness*. The Hebrew story of Adam and Eve isn't about how they chose hate over love; it's a story about how they chose *self* over love. The opposite of love is living a life that is all about you. The opposite of love is placing *me* before *we* and *I* before *us*. The opposite of love is living a life using others as a means to *your* end. But living a life of *meaning* is being a means to an end that is not *you*.

Because I have yet to see a story of how

Greed,

Materialism,

Or pride

Create a better world.

Have you?

But when I've seen someone use the power of technology to reunite a homeless man to his family that he hasn't seen in twenty years,[67]

When I've seen someone stand against racial injustice,

When I've seen people generously give their lives to build an orphanage in Kenya,

When I've seen a person sit with someone battling depression and say, "I'm with you."

In those moments, I felt like I caught a glimpse of heaven.

The iWorld has only enough space for you, but becoming a means to somebody else's end creates a world big enough for everyone. God's final promise to Abraham was that, when he followed life where it was calling him, it would not lead him to an iWorld that was only big enough for him. The endgame wasn't just Abraham's benefit. But life was calling him into a world that was big enough to create blessing and belonging for all people on earth.

While Genesis 12 says a lot about a promise, it says even more about the Promise Maker. Genesis 12 gives us an idea of how God works and what God's ultimate intentions are for the world. Genesis 12 tells us that God is always creating a world where everyone belongs.

God is actively putting the world together.

God is seeking to bless all people, not just some people.

Which means if you are creating a future that isn't big enough for everyone, a life where you are the center, and a life that is about being blessed instead

---

67 Check out an incredible organization called Miracle Messages (www.miraclemessages.org) who have leveraged technology to reunite the homeless with their families and loved ones.

of being a blessing, then you are not creating the world that God is creating. Any version of the future that is divided, selfish, greedy, and doesn't create room for everyone is not compatible with the world that God is making and should be rejected as quickly as possible. God's final promise to Abraham should remind us that true life is always leading you to love, so if your life isn't leading you to love, then you've settled for a cheap knockoff of life instead of the real thing.

The story of Abraham should remind us all that fully loving and fully living are not only synonymous but exactly the journey that true life is inviting us into.

The noted missionary writer Don Richardson refers to the first two promises in Genesis 12 as the top line ("I will bless you") and the final promise as the bottom line ("and you will be a blessing"). The blessings we receive from God are the top line, not the bottom line. The bottom line is that God is using your life for the cause of love and creating a future where everyone can be blessed and everyone can belong. I often wonder if we're in danger of concentrating so much on the top line—all the good things God has given us—that we forget the bottom line: that we are blessed to be a blessing.

I think this is why we, including myself, have a tendency to overcomplicate the idea of *calling*.

As a pastor, I counsel a lot of people who struggle with this. Self-help books and conferences are a booming industry. We're all craving calling and meaning. So I'm constantly finding myself being asked how does one discover and activate their calling? What if they get their calling wrong? What if they miss their calling and come to the end of their life full of regret?

I wonder if we have made calling far more complex than it was ever meant to be?

I wonder if we've actually transformed this beautiful and selfless picture of calling that we see here with Abraham into just a socially acceptable form of narcissism?

Because what I have often found humming underneath the question "What is my calling?" is a person that is still living in the iWorld. They still haven't quite left their land, birthplace, and father's house because underneath this question often is an intention that is still very self-centered. It's easy to become an accidental narcissist when you've only ever lived in and known the iWorld.

But if Abraham's story teaches us something about not only *how* life calls us but *where* life calls us, then we should find it interesting that the final destination of this journey Abraham was being invited on wasn't a life of self-centeredness, vanity, or fame for the sake of fame. We see through Abraham's story that the endgame of life is *love*. Life is calling you to be a means to somebody else's end. Life is calling you to create a future where more people can be blessed and belong in the world than before.

Calling in the iWorld asks, "*What* am I here for?"

But when life calls you, it invites you to ask, "*Who* am I here for?"

Frederick Buechner put it this way: "Calling is the place where your deep gladness and the world's deep hunger meet."

I wonder if the reason you have found yourself stuck when it comes to calling is because you've been asking the wrong question? I wonder what new possibilities and ideas might begin to open up for you when you begin to move from *what* you are here for to first asking *who* am I here for? I wonder what skill that brings you great joy could be used to satisfy the hunger of someone else? How could you become a means to an end that is not you?

This reminds me of a story I heard about how an old woman with cupcakes started a brothel chaplaincy agency in Australia. Jan was sixty-six at the time, and she was living in a nice suburb in Melbourne. But Jan found herself in a bit of a dilemma. Jan's phone number was only two digits different from the phone number of the brothel in her neighborhood. She kept getting awkward calls when people mixed up the numbers.

It was, as you could imagine, disturbing her and her husband, and Jan decided that she was going to change her number. But on the day that she was going to change her number, while she was praying, she felt the Lord speak to her. She felt God challenge her: "Why are you changing your number, Jan?" She told God about how the calls were disturbing her. But she couldn't shake the feeling that life was calling her to reconsider and to begin to think differently about this situation.

By the way, Jan's story is another reminder for all of us. That just like it was for Abraham and just like it was for Jan, before God calls you, he often *disturbs* you with something that is broken in the world. If you want to see where God might be leading you, start with the brokenness in the world that creates a brokenness in you. Start with the thing that makes you slam your fist on the table. Start with the brokenness in the world that causes you to say, "Someone should do something about that."

Because perhaps, that someone is *you*.

Back to Jan.

That day, Jan decided to do something about this situation. She talked with a friend and asked what she thought she should do. Her friend asked her what she would do if a new neighbor moved in? She responded that it would be normal for her to take over some cupcakes and introduce herself, asking how she could help.

So her friend told her, "What if we did that? What if we did what you know how to do best?"

So that day Jan decided to stick with what she loved doing. She would bake some cupcakes, and she would go over to the brothel and introduce herself. Just like she would normally do.

Jan didn't wait for a professional to go to the brothel.
She didn't wait for someone else to start a program.
Jan decided to *be* the program.

It is worth reminding us today that, while it is not bad to pray for a move from God, God's plan is for *you* to be the move from God. God's Plan A is people. You are the program God is using to create a world of blessing where everyone can belong. So don't pray for a movement from God until you're willing to be a part of that movement.

Because when you pray for purpose, God sends you to people.

So Jan walked to the brothel, armed with cupcakes; she went up the steps and knocked on the door. One of the brothel managers came to the door to ask what she wanted (As Jan was not the normal clientele). Jan was so nervous, everything she planned on saying went out the window, so she simply shoved the cupcakes forward and said, "I brought cupcakes!"

No one could've predicted what happened next.

The manager invited Jan inside to meet the women; Jan was able to tell them that she was a neighbor who saw them and wanted to get to know them as they shared a cupcake together. It was unbelievable. Jan exited that brothel floating ten feet off the ground.

But the story gets even better.

Fast-forward with me about eight years. There is now a network of brothel visitation teams across the nation of Australia. All of these teams are armed with cupcakes, and they bring relationship, connection, hope, and the possibility of freedom with them every week to women trapped in prostitution.

How amazing is that?

So before you list out all the reasons why you can't follow life where it is calling you, let me remind you that, if a sixty-six year old with cupcakes can fight prostitution in her country, then you can do whatever life is inviting you to do also.

But it begins with you asking, "Who am I here for?" Followed by the next question: "What passions do I have that can be used to satisfy the need of someone else?" Remember, calling is where your deep gladness and the world's deep hunger meet.

Which means that, whether you bake cupcakes, crunch numbers, make lattes, run a company, mop floors, or are a stay-at-home parent, student, or engineer—what matters most is not *what* you do but *who* you are doing it for and *why*. If Abraham's story shows us that life is always leading you to love, then that calling is less about *arriving* and far more about *deciding*.

Calling is less about arriving at the corner office and more about deciding who you'll love while you're still in the cubicle. It's less about arriving to a certain status one day and more about deciding who you can serve this day. When calling is about arriving, you will live a life of striving. But when you see that calling is about deciding, you will go from striving to serving.

You'll go from living a life that is always *looking* to a life that is always *loving*.

If you're wrestling with what life might be calling you into, God's final promise to Abraham should prod some new questions, the kind you'd never ask in the iWorld.

Questions like the following: What big or small thing can I contribute to human flourishing? What can I do that would be good for the earth? What skills that bring me joy can I use for the good for my city, my nation, my world? How can I make the world a place where everyone can belong? If that's too big of a question, then ask how you can make the world a little bit bigger and a little bit more of a blessing for one more person. What work could you do that would make God smile? What work can you do that, after you do it, will cause you to hear God whisper in your ear, "Well done?"

Kabbalistic wisdom talks of two different types of vessels for God's creative energy. Some are containers, open at the top and closed at the bottom. They allow the power of life to flow in but do not let it flow out of the other end. The other type of vessels, though, have decided to serve as conduits for divinity; they were not stopped up at the bottom. The power of life flowed in on one side and out from the other side. Those vessels that received but did not give ultimately self-destructed; they shattered from the abundance of good that they tried to contain within themselves. It is only those who passed on what they received that were part of an interconnective network on both ends, fulfilled their function, and were able to serve God's creative purpose.

This goes for us as well—we must take a cue from the vessels of creation. No true good can be enjoyed without passing it on. We too must be open-ended vessels. Blessings are not meant to just flow into us but rather to flow *through* us.

A person should always ask themselves, "Is the world a bit of a better place today because of me? Has my existence added anything to the sum total of blessing in the world?" We compute our carbon imprint, and our ecological footprint causes us to pause, and that is a good thing. But these concerns are all about mitigating harm. Life invites us to go beyond that and seek ways to not just prevent damaging the world but also actively participate in *repairing* the world. To create a bigger world where blessing and belonging for all is made possible.

For some of you, this might mean that life is calling you out of a job that only perpetuates the iWorld. Like the fast-fashion industry that makes a profit at the expense of people. Or any work that diminishes humans into sexual objects. Or maybe you are a pastor and working for a church that is only interested in building a brand instead of caring for the marginalized. Or perhaps you work for a company that relentlessly exploits the earth's natural resources jeopardizing the wellbeing of future generations. That work is iWorld work, and it's not the work that creates a bigger and better world for all people.

For others of you, perhaps what needs to change isn't *what* you do but how and *why* you do what you do. You don't need a new job, you need a new *perspective*.

You don't need different work as much as you need to begin to work *differently*.

To follow life when it calls is to find your role in the building of a bigger and better world that fights for humanity, justice, harmony, fulfillment, and delight. That is your work, and far too many people have missed life when it calls because they have traded their *work* for their *job*. They've traded the wonder of purpose for the security of a paycheck. Far too many people have settled for making a *living* when they were created to make a *life*. Your work is to take the thing that brings you deep joy and bring it to a place where there is deep hunger. And that work doesn't have to wait to start someday; it is your work that life is calling you into *today*.

Are you with me?

One last thing.

I think the final promise of Abraham is not only a promise that Abraham will live a life of purpose for the world but also a promise that Abraham's life will become *proof* of what is possible when someone decides to follow life out of the iWorld and into the new world that God is creating.

Because we have so much proof as to what kind of world greed creates.

Unfortunately, we have way too much proof of what kind of world narcissism creates.

And we do not lack proof of what kind of world hate creates.

But Abraham's life is different because his life would become proof of what *love* could create.

Abraham's life would prove that, when you follow life as it calls, you will find yourself participating in the creation of a new world of blessing and belonging for all people.

And I don't know about you, but I think we are in dire need of people whose lives become proof of what love is capable of.

Why not you?
Why not now?
Why not here?

Is your life evidence to others of what love is capable of doing?

God promises Abraham that, if he follows life where it is leading him, if he will listen to the voice that bids him to *Lech-Lecha*, to go and take the inward journey and leave behind the world he has only known, Abraham would encounter a world that he never knew was possible—an ever-expanding world where all people are blessed and everyone belongs. Abraham was being invited into a new world, and God's final promise was that, if he boldly followed life into this new world, Abraham's life would become proof to the world that you could live a life that would outlive your life and the world would be better because of it.

And your life can be proof of the same thing.

You can live a life that will outlive your life, and you can live a life that will create blessing and belonging for others.

Polish designer Korczak Ziolkowski once asked this question: "When your life is over, the world will ask you only one question: 'Did you do what you were supposed to do?'"

That's not just a good question. I think that is *the* question. Did you do what you were supposed to do? It cannot be answered with words. This is a question that must be answered with your life. In the end, how will your life demonstrate your response to that question?

With that said, I'll leave you with this beautiful quote from St. Francis:

"Keep a clear eye toward life's end. Do not forget your purpose and destiny as God's creature. What you are in his sight is what you are and nothing more. Remember that when you leave this earth, you can take nothing that you have received...but only what you have given; a full heart enriched by honest service, love, sacrifice, and courage."

Yes and amen. I couldn't have said it any better.

Chapter 19

Abraham Departed

"So Abraham departed as the Lord had instructed."—Genesis 12:4–4

"That small step in the right direction may end up becoming the biggest step of your life."—Unknown

Six years.

That is how long it has taken me to get this book out of my soul and onto paper.

I cannot even begin to count the number of coffees, Coke Zeros, and hours staring at that stupid and condescending blinking line on my computer. While writing a book about the existential journey that God calls us on, I have had to take that same journey myself in order to complete this book.

Six years ago, the story of this seventy-five-year-old Mesopotamian man had sparked a fire inside of my bones that I have not been able to put out. By the way, I think that's how you know when life is calling you somewhere. I think when life calls you somewhere, it is less like getting a map dropped in your lap and much more like a *match* that sparks a fire in your soul. So many people are looking for a map when they need to be looking for the *match*. If you want to find where life is calling you, perhaps the best place to start is with whatever lights a fire in your soul.

I wonder if that's what it was like for Abraham that evening under the stars when life called him to *Lech-Lecha*.

I wonder if it felt like a fire was burning in his veins. Was that how he knew he had to explore? It's the only way this makes sense to me—because how else do you leave every instinct you have behind, break the rules of your tribe, and walk away from those mindsets that you have built over seventy-five years of life unless something very deep and very real is sparked inside of you that you feel with every fiber of your being?

And that is my hope with writing this book. I did not hope to present to you some neat and tidy map that offers five steps to having an awesome life. We already have shelves stocked up with books like that, and honestly, those books bore me. I didn't want to write that book because I actually believe you are closer to where life is calling you than you might even think. I believe that some of you are perhaps one decision away from a totally different life. And what you don't need is a map; what you do need is a match.

My hope is that this book and the story of Abraham might spark something within you to depart from where you are in order to reach where you must be. There are far too many people settling for where they *can be* instead of pursuing where they *must be*.

I think this is why Abraham's journey to *Lech-Lecha*, to "go to himself," has resonated in three different religions and millions of people for thousands of years. Because, as I have said before, Abraham's journey is, in a lot of ways, a symbol that represents *all of our* journeys. Sure, maybe some of us are called to travel further than others, but if we are to follow life where and when it calls, we all must leave behind some aspect of ourselves to continue to grow and make the long trek inward. You cannot do what you've always done and think as you've always thought and expect to do things that you've never done. I think Abraham resonates with us because we understand what it means to leave behind something familiar so we can become the truest versions of ourselves. Abraham blazed the trail so that we could go and do the same.

Some of us relate to this because we followed life when it called and have experienced the same provision, protection, and purpose that Abraham received.

While others of us relate to Abraham's story because we know what that deep sense of regret feels like—because, like Terah, we settled too soon. We became settlers when we were always meant to be pioneers.

But no matter what camp you find yourself in, I hope that the story of Abraham can create a new hope for all of you: if life called this seventy-five-year-old man to an inward journey of self-discovery, there is still time for us to do the same. Whether you are a student in college, a parent, or grandparent, Abraham's story can remind you that it's never too late to follow life when it calls. If you have a pulse, then you have a purpose.

And this leads to one final question that I wrestled with for quite a while.

Have you ever wondered *why* Abraham was even picked by God in the first place?

Like, what did he do to merit such a beautiful invitation to *Lech-Lecha* from God? What made Abraham qualified for such a task? Why Abraham?

Do I know the answer to that question?

Nope.

And it's not that I haven't looked for that answer. But the Torah is also completely silent on this. At no point do we get any sort of explanation for why Abraham was chosen.

That used to really bother me, but then I realized that maybe that is sort of the point.

I bet that, if we were to learn that Abraham had a certain level of credentials and a stacked resume in order to receive such a call, then we would begin to disqualify ourselves from following in his footsteps. We would begin to grade ourselves against Abraham and sabotage the journey God wants us to take. So it almost feels like the author behind the story of Abraham understands this about humans and doesn't want to give us the opportunity to sabotage our story. Instead, we're given zero reasons why Abraham was picked because the author wants all of us to know that God doesn't look at people the way that we do. Abraham's story was an invitation to see yourself how God has always seen you, and it is a story about how to follow life when it calls.

Jewish history begins with an invitation to travel the long journey inward, and when you do, you will reach a new land, and that new land would be your truest self.

But this book would have never been written, this story would have never been told, and that annoying song in Sunday School about Abraham and his many sons would have never been sung had Abraham stayed where he was. If Abraham had followed in the footsteps of his father Terah and settled where he was, then Abraham would have forever missed where he was always meant to be.

But the good news is that Genesis 12 tells us that "Abraham departed."

At some point, Abraham couldn't stand still any longer.

He couldn't talk about taking the journey anymore.

At some point, he had to put one foot in front of the other and depart from where he was if he was ever going to reach where he was always meant to be. It reminds me of one of my favorite quotes from Walt Disney, another person who used his life as an act of creativity that has changed the world. Walt Disney said, "The way to get started is to quit talking and start doing." That's what Abraham did, and it was the only difference between him and Terah. While Terah stayed, Abraham departed, and he never looked back.

I wonder if right now it is your turn to do the same.

It's your turn to close this book, to make your move, and to start your journey.

Because just as life called Abraham, I am thoroughly convinced that life is calling you. It is why I have spent over six years trying to find the right way to tell you.

Potential is purpose that hasn't been born, and you were never meant to die with your potential. You were meant to squeeze every bit of purpose out of your life until you have nothing left to give.

Abraham followed life, and his story gives us all permission to do the same. His life became a courageous act that can help all of us act courageous. I'm not suggesting the world needs you to be Abraham. But the world desperately needs you to be *you*, and it is you, the real, beautiful, bursting-with-promise you that life is inviting you to discover fully.

There's an ancient rabbinic saying that's worth quoting here. The legendary Rabbi Zusya said this: "In the coming world, they will not ask me: 'Why were you not Moses?' They will ask me: 'Why were you not Zusya?'"

Your job isn't to fit into some mold or prove something to the world; it's to unlock who God's made *you* to be and then go be that in order to create a better world where all can belong.

And that, my friend, is the journey that life is calling you into, and I am convinced that God will protect you and provide for you and that your life will be driven with great purpose, so much so that God will use your life as proof of what is possible when someone follow life where it calls.

I always thought Abraham's journey was about arriving, but it was about something far more beautiful—it was, and has always been, about *becoming*.

And that same voice that called Abraham thousands of years ago as he stood in the desert underneath the stars. That whisper that spoke into his heart and said, "*Lech-Lecha*; go to yourself and leave behind your instincts, the rules of the tribe, and your long-held mindsets, so that I can show you, *you*."

That same whisper is calling you to take the same journey.

Do you hear it?

Will you stay where you are?

Or will you depart and see where life takes you?

Acknowledgements

Where do I begin?

There have been so many people who have walked with me throughout this journey. But the one who I want to thank first is my amazing wife, Jena. You championed me when I felt like giving up, and you always encouraged and empowered me to continue writing until I finished the book. Even though, at times, this meant you were making sacrifices. Words cannot describe how grateful I am for you. Without you, this book doesn't get written.

I also want to thank my OG Community Group. You know who you are. Many years ago, I told you that I was writing this book, and I am grateful for your patience and encouragement as I slowly completed it. You all have shown me what true friendship looks like, and I genuinely am very thankful for each of you in my life.

To the additional family and friends who allowed me to process the book with you and who provided feedback and encouragement and would remember to ask me, "how's the book coming?" Thank you. Whether you knew it or not, you were keeping me accountable and focused on getting this book out of my soul.

Over the past six years, I have drunk an ungodly amount of coffee to finish. Shout out to all of the baristas who kept the coffee coming. Also, Diet Coke. Thank you.

Lastly, I want to thank *you*, the reader. I may not know you or your story, but I hoped that I could write something that you would not only read but even more, that would *read you*. I am so thankful that you would take the time to go on this journey with me, and I hope it was helpful for you. I would love to hear from you and get to know your story more and hear where life is calling you. So feel free to shoot me an email at travclark1986@gmail.com.

Until next time,
Travis Clark